MANNHEIM

MANNHEIM

A Humorous and Unexpected Journey of Self-discovery

A memoir by

CHARLES R. LEVINE

MILL CITY PRESS

Mill City Press, Inc.
2301 Lucien Way #415
Maitland, FL 32751
407.339.4217
www.millcitypress.net

Unless otherwise indicated, Scripture quotations taken from the King James Version (KJV) –*public domain.*

Printed in the United States of America.

Cover design by David Saccheri.

Also available as an ebook.

Some proceeds from this book will go to the ALS Association.

ISBN-13: 978-1-54564-655-7 (Paperback)

Also available in:
ISBN- 978-1-54564-656-4 (Hardcover)
ISBN- 978-1-54564-657-1 (EBook)

THE CONTENTS

"It's easier to build strong children than to repair broken men."
Fredrick Douglas

AUTHOR'S NOTE

In June 1968, I boarded a silver Lockheed C-69 airplane in Travis Air Force Base for the sixteen-hour flight to Mannheim, Germany. It was the start of the nearly fifty-year journey to get out of my own way and become myself. That is the subject of this book.

INDUCTION

W hen I was twenty-four, I believed I had learned more from my successes than my failures. Over the next fifty years, I found out how wrong I had been. My biggest failure, not avoiding the army draft, proved my greatest success.

At the time—it was 1968—my girlfriend, Sharon, and I lived in Hollywood, a pleasant enough time until the shattering day the United States Army sent me its greetings. It was at the height of the Vietnam War, and I never saw Sharon again.

Two weeks later, I stood in line with a bunch of other nude men at the Oakland Army Induction Center. The results of the next three hours would determine the course of my life for the next two years.

"Piss into the bottle and don't switch bottles with anyone," a sergeant ordered us all.

The room was large and cold and had no windows. Fluorescent lights hummed. A radiator rattled, its burdened inflow clattering within the wall. The air stank of the unwashed. Three corporals sat like Caucasian triplets behind metal desks in the center of the room. Their olive-drab shirts were starched cardboard rigid. Brass buttons ran down their fronts. The soldiers' sole job was to assign a position to each man.

I had earlier avoided the draft by joining the National Guard but had failed to attend the required one-weekend-a-month meetings. The military caught up with me within a year. I had a choice: either report for service or dodge the draft. In other words, I could lose my freedom to the army, or to a prison.

"Keep it moving. Move it. Fall in. Keep it moving," a sergeant named Jones ordered. His only task, it seemed, was to keep the cattle moving toward the slaughterhouse.

The wire basket I carried held my belongings, clothes and all, and grew heavier as I awaited the determination of my fate. The man behind me introduced himself.

"I'm Doug," he said, and as I turned he extended his hand. He smelled like pot. "I'm from Berkeley."

"I'm Charles." I kept both hands on my basket.

"So, what do you think of all this, Charlie? That your piss? I smuggled in cat piss, and a bar of soap," seemingly apropos of nothing.

Contrary to orders, he still had on his boxers. "I ain't showin' these guys my hardware," he said. "I don't show no dude my works." I turned back around.

"Hey man, you got anything to eat? Give you half my soap for a candy bar. It's Lifebuoy. You put it in your pits. It'll lower your blood pressure. They'll think you got typhoid or something."

We took a step forward. There was one man ahead of me. He was conspicuously nervous.

"Might I have a word in private, sir?" he asked one of the triumvirate of corporals. "It's a personal matter. I, uh,—"

The corporal looked up at him. "This ain't a confessional, son."

The man leaned closer in, his voice now hushed.

"What is it? You gotta take a shit? Tough, there ain't no toilets in the Nam!"

He gave the recruit his packet back. "Next."

The corporal had an exceptional, if inadvertent, ability to foster images. I stepped forward with a new thought about Nam, which I couldn't have found on a map at gunpoint: There were no toilets there.

I handed him my packet, which he opened.

"You Levine, Charles R.? D.O.B. four, nine, forty four?"

"Isn't that what it says?"

"That your fuckin' name or not?" He gave me a look and pulled on his Lucky Strike. He thumbed through a binder, and filled in a blank on my info sheet. "You're now in the Seventh Cavalry, Levine, Charles R. Next!"

"What does that mean?"

"You're a foot soldier. Your Military MOS is tanker, reconnaissance scout, or machine gunner. Your next stop is Fort Ord for eight weeks of boot camp. Then you go to AIT at Fort Knox, where you'll learn how to kill gooks."

I had read the Handbook of Military Psychology, looking for an out. It read: "... screen out the unfit, select individuals with needed abilities, and place people in jobs most appropriate both to their skills and military needs." Skill sets that inductees might have brought from civilian life could be ignored. I was SOL.

I could throw a baseball hard. That was my only skill, one I supposed the army might see as valuable when it came to pitching hand grenades.

"What determines which it is?"

"God and me. And not in that order."

"I need to see a psychiatrist."

"Tell it to the medic. Follow the black arrows on the floor to the next station."

He handed back my packet and again yelled, "Next!"

I had taken several steps in that direction when I heard a voice from behind.

"Hey Charlie, what about that swap?"

I looked down and followed the arrows.

The doctor's office was barely adequate. So were his test procedures. Dr. Conklin shared a cubicle with two other physicians. There was no privacy. Another recruit and I were checked out together. A poke and a prod and Conklin told me to turn my head and cough. He took my temperature and listened to my heart, measured my height and weight and checked my hearing. He didn't ask for my bottle of urine. With bland indifference, he pronounced me "fit as a fiddle" and told me to put on my clothes. Hence, another step taken in the catastrophe of my twenty-fifth year.

"Report to the supply clerk," he told me.

"I need to see a psychiatrist."

"Get dressed. Next!"

It was not yet noon, and already it had been a long day.

THE LONGEST RIDE

M y morning had begun before dawn. My mother, Kathyren, had dropped me at the Sacramento Greyhound depot, a homeless hangout where many a hobo was given what police used to call "Greyhound therapy,—a ticket outta here, and don't come back, bub." I entered through the garage. Three old Greyhounds sat side by side, their engines idling. All read: OAKLAND. Dozens of loud, young men milled about inside the terminal. Talk of war replaced little sentences of lesser subjects. Men assumed this was their first leg on a trip to Vietnam. Eventually, I boarded one of the buses. The coach was hot and muggy, and I opened my window as far as it would allow.

I sat alone in the last row. An exposed coil spring nicked my left calf as I lowered myself onto the seat. We sat for half an hour, burnt diesel finding its way inside. Conversation died. Eventually we pulled out, heading west on Highway 80 across the Yolo Causeway over the eponymous floodplain. The first rays of daylight glinted off water below. A breeze raised small waves.

I had in my hand a sack lunch. I wondered what Kathyren felt while packing my final meal, a tuna sandwich and an apple. My father had left when I was six, and she had devoted the next eighteen years to me. Now I, too, was leaving her.

As a child, I never felt at home in Sacramento, the modest suburban town bordered by the still smaller hamlets of Roseville and Elk Grove. I had wild ideas about life elsewhere. I was finally leaving, but with an unwanted complication. I had seen my departure to be voluntary, not forced by government order. My future was about to unfold in the hands of other people.

I sought to distract myself from my increasingly pensive gloom. I leaned forward and pulled the blue Greyhound ticket from my

5

back pocket. The fine print read: "Round-trip fares limited to one year." The black box marked Special Endorsements wasn't checked. I had never been a particularly observant Jew, but now thoughts came to mind of the European faithful bound, unknowingly, for Auschwitz or one of the many other death camps.

They, too, had faced a forced and uncertain future. While the context differed, the result for many of us would be the same—death. They were the victims of a pathological dictator; we the victims of fallible faith in America's right to dictate to the world. America's boys were perishing needlessly. Odds were that three of the fifty men on our bus would be wounded or dead when it was all said and done. The odds were ninety times greater than those of drawing a Dead Man's Hand in poker. I looked out the window to wildflowers carpeting the land here and there like scattered throw rugs dyed all the hues of Joseph's coat—yet the beauty was lost on me at that moment.

I was as good as gone and envisioned my funeral: The service delivered in the Evangelical United Brethren Church—my mother was not Jewish—just outside Sacramento. I was pleased to see there were a good number of mourners, some even wiping away tears. An organ played. Take Me Out to the Ballgame replaced Chopin's usual Funeral March in C minor. The bereaved sang along:

"Buy me some peanuts and Cracker Jack. I don't care if I never get back ..."

The minister approached the pulpit and cleared his throat twice before addressing the bereaved.

"Dearly beloved, we are gathered here to honor Chuck. He got shot in the back by 'friendly fire' and was captured by Vietnamese children, who turned him over to the enemy. The barbarians tortured our friend and son for two years—give or take. We're fairly certain our dear son, Private Chuck, didn't reveal anything important; he'd been kept pretty much in the dark. 'Need to know' and all that. Now, he has been enlisted in the army of God. Cookies and beverages will be served in the lobby after the service. Mrs. Levine, please visit the accountant's office before leaving."

Eulogies followed:

Mr. Purdy, my high school English teacher, spoke first: "Chuck sat in the back of class, when he showed up."

"He had a rifle arm," my baseball coach, Del Bandy, volunteered, "but he never could hit the curveball."

"We spent three wonderful weekends together," Sharon added. "He seemed like an alright kinda guy."

"I miss my son dearly," Kathyren said, "although I did have to push him to mow the lawn every single week of his life."

"From what I remember of him, he was tall for his age," my father volunteered.

I saw the inscription on my tombstone:

"Charles R. Levine, born April 9, 1944, died Sept. 2, 1968. He liked the Dodgers—and tuna fish."

The bus bounced over a pothole and startled me back to reality. A few others similarly woke only to doze off minutes later. I admired their resignation. We were now an hour closer to Oakland, and I quit thinking of my looming death. It was a given.

NOT CRAZY ENOUGH

I pulled from my pocket my last bid to escape fateful Vietnam, a mental evaluation from a Los Angeles psychologist named Miriam. She and I had planned my draft exemption for months. I had considered pursuing a religious out, prior to meeting her, but there were irresolvable problems:

The universe is thirteen point eight billion years old, with one hundred billion galaxies, each containing one hundred billion stars or so. Ten thousand billion stars, some of them suns. Science does not know where any of this came from. No one knows. Man's origin is a mystery. Another of life's great questions: Why did God let Hitler's parents successfully make love? These mysterious befuddlements would have made arguing my way out of the service, based on religion, with a straight face, impossible. Miriam's liberal thinking, however, matched her flexible ethics, and better suited my needs.

I read her letter for at least the tenth time:

"PSYCHOLOGICAL EVALUATION

"IDENTIFYING AND BACKGROUND DATA: The patient is a 24-year-old male Caucasian. He is an only child, the product of divorced parents. The patient lived alone with his mother until age 20 before leaving home to attend college. The patient suffers from pervasive developmental disorder and attention deficit hyperactivity. He has problems with motivation. There is a history of difficulty in social situations. He was under the care of another psychologist for two months prior to coming here. Symptoms have included difficulty sustaining attention, not seeming to listen when addressed, failure to finish tasks, difficulty with organization, avoiding tasks requiring sustained mental effort, losing things, being distracted by extraneous stimuli, being forgetful.

"DIAGNOSES: AXIS I: Major depression, recurrent/moderate. AXIS II: No diagnosis. AXIS III: No diagnosis, histrionic features. AXIS IV: Occupational problems, other psychosocial and environmental problems. AXIS V: Current GAF: 41-50. Highest in the past year: 48.

"PROGNOSIS:

"The patient will likely have further substantial deterioration of psychosocial functioning.

"RECOMMENDATIONS: The patient will benefit only from ongoing supportive psychotherapy, and at this time should remain on his current regimen, which includes monitoring while on a suitable, heavy dosage of Clozapine."

Although she had had not included my suggestion to add something about my doctor-assisted suicide inquiry, any rational reader had to accept her assessment.

Two MPs escorted me from Dr. Conklin's cubicle to a small office. A sign on the door read: Psychosocial Issues, Lt. Cole. The room did not resemble my psychologist's relaxing office. An acoustically porous wall separated us from a bathroom, muffled voices, and a chaotic chorus of flushing. Lt. Cole sat in the only chair, behind a grey steel-case desk. There was nothing on his desk save for a cup of coffee. The walls were similarly bare, save for a poster of Uncle Sam pointing an accusatory finger at me. He wanted me far more than I wanted anything to do with him.

Lt. Cole was younger than me. I stood before him, my judge, jury, and potential executioner. I still clutched my sealed specimen of urine. The MPs stood beside me, their well-muscled arms crossed. Cole tugged at a stubborn drawer and addressed me without looking up.

"What's on your mind, Levine?"

"I'm a sick man, doctor."

The lieutenant's drawer finally yielded, and he removed a silver Zippo and a pack of Marlboros. He tamped the pack on the back of his wrist and pulled one out and wristed open the lighter. His thumb spun the rough-surfaced wheel against the flint.

"Smoke 'em if ya got 'em," he invited, without offering me one.

A clerk walked in, and Cole told me to hand him my specimen. I did and handed Cole my file and psychological evaluation. He seemed to take interest in the evaluation. He rocked back in his squeaky chair and stared at me.

"What are you qualified to do, Levine?"

"Not much," I assured him, "other than playing baseball." I told him the army would be far better off without me and my ilk. I explained my empathy for the beleaguered Vietnamese and their decades-long struggle against would-be colonizers. I told him of my admiration for Uncle Ho, my words punctuated by the non-stop flushing next door. I explained to him how the war—thanks to JFK's and LBJ's mistakes—could not be won, in any event. Lt. Cole said not a word.

I informed him of ethical and moral principles, augmented by a little Kantian theory. I spoke of our moral obligation to respect the dignity of all people and that that has meaning only when we protect central human interests by granting them a status ethically superior to mere wants, and that when my wants exceed your wants, the market goal of seeking the optimal satisfaction of wants is attractive so long as the conflict does not involve rights. In which case, rights trump mere desires and should not be sacrificed, even if doing so would maximize the overall good.

Nodding and clearly unperturbed, Cole blew a perfect smoke ring. We watched the circle drift for a long moment. Finally, he looked up at me.

"You're the third man who has informed me of that today, Levine."

Cole jotted a note, slipped it into a separate file, then rub-ber-stamped mine.

I have to say in his favor, he was polite and patient in listening to my failed effort to maneuver my way out of harm's way.

"I thank you as I thanked them. Now, report to Room Nine to be sworn in."

I realized too late that I should've headed immediately to Canada.

The guards began to escort me out as Cole addressed me again: "Baseball, huh?"

"Yep," I said, as the guards led me out of the cubicle.

Fifteen or so fellow recruits faced a stage in Room Nine. Another group milled around until an officer in dress uniform entered and stood behind the podium; polished brass insignia identified him as a major.

A kaleidoscope of service ribbons adorned his left breast. I wondered what they represented. I considered decorations for civilian behavior: Good Dietary Habits, a crossed silver knife and fork on a green background; Virtue, an eggless nest, on white; Old Age, A rusty helmet on a silver background. "Raise your right hands," he said. "Repeat after me: I, state your name, do solemnly swear that I will support and defend the Constitution of the United States against all enemies, foreign and domestic; that I will bear true faith and allegiance to the same; and that I will obey the orders of the President of the United States and the orders of the officers appointed over me, according to regulations and the Uniform Code of Military Justice. So help me God."

I raised my hand but didn't utter a word. My youthful Cub Scout experience had turned me off on oaths. I had no intention of honoring the army Oath of Enlistment, even in the eyes of God. Private Charles R. Levine now had to summon the energy to survive the next eighteen months. I blamed myself for the circumstances. I could not deny the facts that had led to my induction. I skipped Guard meetings and got caught. I skipped college classes and got caught. Had I skipped the country, I likely would have got caught, as well. Stupefied, I stood there, hand raised, because of decisions I had made. The consequences were predictable. Civilian life was behind, military life ahead. This was a transitional moment.

THE PHILADELPHIA PHILLIES

After Basic Training, I reported to Armored Forces Headquarters in Fort Knox, Kentucky, for Advanced Military Training. I remembered living freely with a woman in California and being enrolled in the Don Martin School of Broadcasting, with an eye on a radio career. Now, I was housed with forty men in Kentucky — and decidedly not free.

There was no privacy at the center of this orderly existence. The barracks were single story and poorly insulated. Bunk beds lined bare walls. Standing lockers separated the bunks. Bunking in a room of snorers at night, and in the company of gun-happy lifers in day, made life miserable. When the lights were off I laid there in the room's blackness with a group of lives so foreign to me that they might have been from another country, another planet. My world had become devalued. Once I crossed the line in Oakland, I was damned to be pulled in deeper and deeper. In short, I was in the game. I tried to live in the past while realizing I was likely soon to be doomed to the hereafter.

Life got darker by the week. The government was fighting a vociferous opposition to the war. We were waging a never declared war, and exactly why remained a mystery, even after its end in 1975.

I had little in common with most of my fellow soldiers. I was older, to begin with. Some of my newfound colleagues could barely read. Many came from rural areas I knew nothing of. Among them was Corporal Delmont Slaycum, a sixteen-year-old enlistee from Appalachia.

Slaycum came from a family of hunter-gatherers. The Slaycums' subsistence largely depended on prey they killed or captured. They hunted or trapped deer, squirrels, and snakes in the hollows of West Virginia.

Slaycum claimed to have nine brothers and six sisters. Parental restraint was absent in his woodsy upbringing. The father lived with "anuder family ovron the next mountin, and mama had a boyfrund down the road." There had been no hierarchy among the males, each of whom owned a "huntin' weapon." These circumstances, no doubt, played a part in what happened to Slaycum.

Slaycum's face was covered with tiny bumps. Someone without hesitation asked him about his apparent malady: "What happened to your face?"

"I played chicken—against my brother."

"That don't answer my question."

"I bet I could throw my knife and stick him before he could get off a round from his twelve gauge."

So it was that Slaycum became known as Leadhead.

Leadhead outranked me by two grades. He might have become my boss. Corporals take command of their units if officers above them are unable to perform their duties. Leadhead, as the ranking soldier, would be obligated to manage the surviving privates if those above him were killed or otherwise disabled in combat. The vision of my fate lying in the hands of the likes of Leadhead was frightening.

With graduation from advanced training a week off, I decided I wouldn't accept deployment to Vietnam under any condition. I began a subversion campaign. I cornered my company commander, a Lt. Baker, and a sergeant. I shared with them lesser versions of my failed induction lecture. I refused to participate in more training. Counter-arguments were peppered with threats of prison and forfeiture of citizenship. I was further threatened with recycling—a repeat of advanced training.

Yet, Baker then, for some unfathomable reason, took a new tack.

"Levine, what merit do you have? What can you do?"

I stayed the course. "I have nothing against Vietnamese," I said. "I find racial slurs against them appalling." I went all in. "In fact, I find young Asian men attractive."

I looked at Baker as intensely as he stared at me, seeming to listen to me with a quiet intelligence before saying, "Levine, you're not getting out with that line of bullshit. You're only making things difficult for yourself. I asked you what can you do?"

I tried being myself, but wasn't getting anywhere. It was then that something more than a minor miracle occurred. I remembered Lt. Cole's parting question, "Baseball, huh?" It turned out that armed forces covet athletes, providing some of us special dispensation. Team sports promoted competitiveness, which, it was believed, nurtured esprit de corps. I decided to become a "Philly."

"I played baseball in the Philadelphia Phillies' organization, sir."

I dropped a few names. I was sure Baker saw through me. Regardless, I felt certain he wanted to rid Fort Knox of me. As it turned out, I was right; I had a new assignment, should I choose to accept it. I did. I became an army baseball player and Baker was rid of his problem.

I was deployed to the 7th Cavalry Division in Mannheim, Germany. I felt relief and that I had beat the system. Philly Chuck broke the rules by finding a clever way to work within them. I assumed that I had "gotten over," a phrase used as cryptic jargon that makes no sense to the world outside the army. Of the forty GIs in my platoon preparing for battle, only I had beat odds and avoided Vietnam deployment. I was headed for Europe, armored in a baseball uniform; no southeast Asia for me. What I hadn't realized was that the baseball season was but three months long. Nor, was I told that the 7th cavalry was a company that transferred GIs to Vietnam.

FIVE DIAMONDS FOR A DOG

I was always "good with numbers," as my third-grade teacher put it, an affirmation that I clung to and came to realize was true.

Club Normandy was a poker room in a marginal area of downtown Sacramento with a sign posted on the door's scratched glass that warned that those under the age of eighteen were not allowed to gamble there. "Penalties Apply." I was seventeen and not only gambled there, I won there.

Back then, in 1961, there were only a handful of card rooms in California. Today, thanks to the Indian Gaming Regulatory Act of 1988, there are eighty-nine legal card rooms in the state and sixty-two casinos. The Normandy was a dump. Cigarette smoke, stale beer and sweat fouled the stagnant air. Five, round, blotched, green-felted tables hosted poker games with eight seats, one or two of which were occupied by house shills. A gabby, tip-dependent waitress served up cheap beer and prepackaged sandwiches. "Just speak up, honey. I can give you potato chips too, at no extra cost." It was important to request a fresh deck every so often, as occasionally a shyster would mark the cards with mustard or ketchup.

My buddy Tom Harris and I were regulars at the Normandy and could win twenty or thirty dollars on a good night. It definitely beat stocking shelves at the Safeway. The game was five-card draw poker, no wild cards. Per house rules, a player could bet no more that he had on the table at the beginning of each hand.

On a late night a few days before Christmas, I locked into battle with a man called Tibby. We were the last two bettors in the hand. I had been dealt the six, seven, eight, and nine of diamonds and drew one card. Tibby drew two. I raised his bet modestly. Tibby called and raised mine. I raised again. Tibby then pushed all his remaining money into the pot and said, "I want to raise you another $20."

"That's a big bet. You got the money?"

"In my wallet."

I called his bet and pushed my chips into the pot. Tibby rose from his seat, slapped his cards face up on the table, and reached for the pot. Of the six hundred forty nine thousand, seven hundred and forty possible poker hand draws, only fifty-seven beat his four kings. My fifth card, the ten of diamonds, gave me one of them, filling the only natural straight flush I had ever seen. I placed my left hand on the back of Tibby's right hand and exposed my cards. With the speed of a paint stroke covering canvas, his face drained from three-beer red to lily white.

"You owe the kitty a couple of sawbucks, Tibby."

Tibby didn't have either. He pulled three or four singles from his wallet and asked if he could pay the rest after the holidays.

I told him we needed to step outside for a business meeting. I had no intention of harming the withered old man. I just wanted his name and address because I knew he wouldn't be seen again at the Normandy. He stuttered an okay and said he could cover the bet with what was in his car. The rest of the players followed us out into the alley, expecting a fight. There wouldn't be one.

Tibby had inside his 1951 Packard 200 three caged brown and white Beagle puppies, one of which I accepted in lieu of cash, and that night brought home Kathyren's Christmas gift, which, after I left for Mannheim, remained her companion for the next decade—the prosaically named "Puppy."

THE FISH'S CURSE

M any of my adult recollections have faded, pale ghosts, but several youthful memories are clear as the day their events occurred: Yellow ducklings waddling in a line behind me at age four. Danny Bosum banging my head against a garbage can, chipping my front teeth at age five. Dad moving away at six. My redubbing myself Chuck at age seven.

The name Chuck, I had decided, would look better on a baseball card than would Charles. Some of the legends had nicknames: George Herman Ruth was Babe; Lawrence Edwin Snider was The Duke; Harold Peter Reese was known as Pee Wee. Charles Rodney Levine would be known as Chuck—at least until I was tagged with something else.

I was Kathyren's only child, and she was my only parent. After dad disappeared, male influence, with the exception of an occasional new uncle, was replaced by sure, steady voices on the radio. Among them, Sam Spade and The Lone Ranger and Gunsmoke's Matt Dillon. These magnificent men shared unflinching determination to achieve justice. The sharp-sighted writers behind them had created audible worlds of make believe, ones into which a little boy could vanish.

Most broadcasts aired after dark, and I disappeared into a universe of verbal fantasy—until I discovered a reality that exceeded Spade and Dillon and The Shadow, Gang Busters and Dragnet, too. One voice rang above them all.

The Sacramento Solons were my hometown Triple-A, Pacific Coast League baseball team, doing incessant battle with San Francisco's Seals, Hollywood's Stars and Portland's Beavers. Every time the Solons played, home or away, the radio brought them to me from reawakening April through fading September.

The Solons' announcer was a master at crafting mental images—even while working his way through a six pack: "Jones swings. He hits a high fly ball to deep center field! It's going, going, gone! Open up a Lucky!" By the seventh-inning, KFBK's Tony Koester might have slightly slurred his description, but I saw the ball rise and the desperate outfielder surrender to inevitability and fans scrap over the souvenir. It was 1953. Nippy "Shoeshine" Jones one night skied a decisive home run into the Portland night, and Koester, not necessarily in celebration, church-keyed yet another can of Lucky Lager Beer—a Solon's sponsor—not that Koester had actually witnessed any of what he was describing; I had no idea that this genius was embellishing on what he took off the wire's tape, the click of his tongue replicating a wood bat's collision with a horsehide-bound ball. He'd slap his thigh to simulate the pop of a hardball impacting a glove.

As far as I knew, the Solon's announcer was in every park. Koester, in fact, called road games from a studio a short bicycle ride from my house. By the time that was made aware to me, it only enhanced my appreciation of his gift. He, of course, wasn't the first practitioner of this vanished art. The practice of recreating baseball games dates to the earliest days of radio. Ronald Reagan re-created Chicago Cub games from a station in Des Moines, Iowa, before he went into acting and politics.

Koester exposed me to baseball. I got roped in by his imagery to the extent that I rarely argued my eight o'clock bedtime. I lay hidden beneath the covers with my transistor radio turned low and Babe, my one-eared, multihued alley cat, curled between my feet. Koester between pitches altered his voice and yelled: "Popcorn, here! Get'yer cold beer here." Background cheers were prere-corded, but not to my knowledge. I was at the game. Koester to this day remains a hero to me.

Life in my formative years centered on sports. Girls were becoming important; studies were a form of forced labor—but sports, sports were everything at the time. I played football in the fall, basketball in the winter and baseball year-round. I made my Little League team, The Sacramento Engineers, at ten.

Our uniforms were white, with crossed blue shovels stitched on the jerseys beneath the sponsor's name. Number 9 was embroidered on my shirt back. Our white hats bore the Engineers' uppercase SE logo. Kathyren bought me a Spaulding catcher's mitt and a pair of rubber spikes. I was a baseball player! My life, at the expense of everything else, was committed to our national pastime.

At twelve, I made an All-Star Team. I felt myself afloat. My ship had left the dock and now was sailing toward the big leagues. I had it all figured out: I'd play for the Brooklyn Dodgers and sign a contract with Topps Bubble Gum, and kids would collect Chuck Levine trading cards along with those featuring Willie and The Duke and that of a young switch-hitter from Commerce, Oklahoma, named Mickey Mantle. Kids clamored for flat packs containing six cards and a slab of bubblegum. I just knew that someday I would be among those greats, the envy of children everywhere. They'd blow bubbles while memorizing the stats off the back of Chuck's baseball card. But first our team had to reach the Little League World Series in Williamsport, Pennsylvania.

One week before our first regional game I went fishing off the banks of the Sacramento River. Good and bad luck happened that day. I caught several small bluegill and one large, feisty carp. While removing a barbed hook from the carp, I jabbed my throwing hand. The wound got infected, doubling my thumb size and keeping me off the field. I was one poor, unhappy creature. If the carp hadn't taken my hook, had I cast my line in another direction, had I used a salmon egg for bait, instead of a worm,—well, now, my big league career was in doubt, at the tender age of 12.

The elimination game was played on a warm Sunday, August 12, 1956. Fans, parents, and friends packed the bleachers. The event was deemed "Sacramento Significant." On Saturday, our team participated in a Senior Citizen's Day parade down Broadway. The Sacramento Bee sent a sports reporter to cover the game. The Kiwanis Club Kid's Band mangled the national anthem, but who cared. Miss Little League, our coach's eight-year-old daughter, tossed out the ceremonial first pitch. His son, Joey Paragallo, took my place on the mound. The game began at 10 a.m. I put on my uniform—I wasn't going to be denied that—and watched disconsolately from the stands.

The end came an hour and half later—the longest ninety minutes of my young life. We had lost. Damned carp. There would be no trip to Williamsport. I might have pitched a no-hitter, or hit the game-winning home run, I was sure, had I only been able to play. I felt responsible for the loss. I was suffering from an imaginary crime—Lincoln might have survived had I stepped between him and Booth, but, no, I'd gone fishing.

The annual Malcolm Hirsch awards dinner was a few weeks later, with several hundred people on hand. The celebration included all sixteen league teams, families, sponsors, and special guests— including Tony Koester! We all wore our uniforms. Parents were dressed to the eights; most could not afford the nines. The league handed out plaques and commemorative gifts to the various Most Valuable Players and to their coaches. Mayor Clarence Azavedo acknowledged businessman Malcolm Hirsch's contributions to the Sacramento Little League program. Azavedo named the first winner of the Malcolm Hirsch Perpetual Award at the end of his speech. The thirty-inch-tall trophy was the final award that evening. It was presented to the player who had best exemplified good sportsmanship throughout the season.

The Mayor removed a piece of paper from an envelope, and said, "Will Chuck Levine please come to the podium?" I couldn't believe my ears. I was nervous and embarrassed. I was going to receive an award for not playing. Those shocking words: "Will Chuck Levine please come to the podium" still buzz in my mind today.

THE NEIGHBORHOOD

The post-war boom—the halcyon 1950s—skipped my South Sacramento neighborhood, yet we as children had simple fun in our world of simple expectations. Parents, meanwhile, labored to put food on the table, let alone to save up for anything as frivolous as a television. Any vacations they might have considered were imaginary. We children lived for recess, for after-school play, for our wonderful, carefree summers. All we really needed was a ball and a bat and a radio.

Buster Brown was a radio mascot, whose tagline always amused me: "Hi, my name is Buster Brown. I live in a shoe. That's my dog Tige. He lives there too." Buster was a wealthy little boy who dressed in girl's clothes, and whose mother flogged him with a stick. My mother never dressed me in drag, although from time to time I did feel the business end of a wooden spoon. No, my alliance with Buster related to his housing. I imagined life in a shoe.

A house can provide an insight into the status, as well as the interests and personality, of the owner. The house at 2740 24th Avenue was less than twenty feet wide by thirty feet deep. It comprised a kitchen—a nook really—a bedroom, and a shared living and sleeping room. The toilet was inside an attached shed. The shoebox shrank each of the next fifteen years as I grew to my full measure of six-feet-two and nearly two hundred pounds.

Yet, we were not destitute. Doubly thrifty is a better description. Kathryen did her best with what she had and with what she didn't have.

Furnishings and interior decoration were modest. Vertical, striped green and yellow paper adorned walls. The floor was concrete. Heat came from an oven. Dishes, clothes, and family were washed in the same sink. Our icebox stood behind the house.

The iceman delivered blocks weekly, more during the blistering Sacramento summers. There was no air conditioning. Our dinnerware was not a matched set. I won a new glass or two each year by pitching nickels into them at the state fair. Sometimes, that endeavor allowed me to come home with a glass bowl, which was repurposed after the goldfish died.

I don't know where the furniture came from. Three chairs— one crippled—a faded brown couch, a wobbly smoking stand, a kitchen card table, and two beds were bought or picked up used. The prize item was an RCA Victor tube radio. The receiver stood thirty-eight inches tall and was wrapped in mahogany veneer. Station indicators were decorated with three horizontal white band labels: International, Domestic, and Special Service. Eight push buttons and four dials beneath balanced the aesthetics. Three of the functions functioned. The on-off button, volume dial, and Special Service knob brought in our reception, domestic programs only. Dad surmised that, "The dumb shits at RCA got the labels mixed up." He threatened to return the radio for a new one or sue the "dumb shits," but he left before the radio did.

My parents had limited childrearing skills. Neither was well educated. As a result, my education was doomed from the first day of kindergarten. I began school in the fall of 1949. I was escorted the two blocks from home to Ethel Phillips Elementary School. Kathyren left me on the playground and went to work. This was my first exposure to a large group. Her effort to prepare me for the occasion failed. I had contracted impetigo, and Kathyren had treated the rash with an azure-colored, topical agent.

I looked like a robin egg with ears. Our neighborhood had white kids and brown kids and yellow kids. Now it had a blue one. I saw a girl gasp at my face and whisper something to another, which caused both to laugh and run off. The school bell rang and all dutifully, albeit reluctantly, marched to class—all but me. I spent the first day of school quarantined, coloring by myself in an office with the door closed.

My parents didn't much understand children, emotions, or money. They were penny wise and tons foolish. Both worked and money was tight; at least school negated the need to pay babysitters.

Jack LaLane, Dwight Eisenhower, Cary Grant, and Marilyn Monroe were names on the national stage in the '50s. Wheatie Krieger, Joey Paragallo, Tykes Thorsted, and Hazel the twin played on the neighborhood stage.

While our house was small, our front lawn of crabgrass accommodated a dozen enthusiastic kids engaged in tag, hide and seek, and ball games. Dwight "Wheatie" Krieger acquired his nickname for his odd practice of pouring Wheaties on everything he ate. Joey Paragallo, a proud Cub Scout, always played in uniform. Tykes had acquired a tremendous record collection of dubious provenance from Tower Records. None of the record covers matched their vinyl contents. I loved Hazel Natural and was fond of her twin, Lucille. Hazel usually brought her cat to the yard in a box with holes. Oddly, no dogs were around. Bonnie Barnes was the recipient of my first kiss, a sneaker, between licks of our shared ice cream cone. The romance didn't last.

Our property was beneath a landing path into Sacramento's Municipal Airport, three miles southwest of where we lived. No planes crashed into the neighborhood before I left home in 1964. One did, however, eight years later. On September 24, 1972, a plane slammed into Farrell's Ice Cream Parlor, and twenty-two people died, including twelve children and nine members of a single family.

Aircraft of all shapes and sizes flew over the house. Fuselage lettering became easier to read as planes increased in size during the years. Boeing jets passing overhead drowned out all other sound. Low-flying Piper Cubs and Cessnas were not so loud, yet still louder than the freight trains squealing as they braked at the end of the block.

I was among the kids who played with trains. We lived out our fantasies of owning model trains, the Lionels and American Flyers and the like. Mine came to life with the Southern Pacific and Western Pacific—real trains. "Stay away from the trains, Charles," was my mother's sage advice, which, of course, I and my friends ignored. Twenty-fourth Avenue led to the tracks, which led to Southern Pacific's freight yards, a mile north. I loved the trains; their sounds, their smell, the danger of their enormity. The tracks became my playground away from home. Detached train cars were ours to explore.

I've broken into scores of cabooses. This was part of my potentially lethal fun with trains, and I loved throwing rocks at passing freight cars, which helped develop my pitching arm. Setting pennies on the track to be further flattened was a favorite pastime. I climbed car ladders and hung on while the trains began to move. Cabooses were the most fun. They were little red houses on wheels, serving as the conductor's office. He could see the boxcars, tankers, flat cars and bold, adventurous little boys from his perch. Breaking into them was a never-ending thrill.

Inside, I usually found treasures. Conductors kept records and conducted business there. Their walls often were decorated with pictures and posters, and items of no interest to anyone but inquisitive boys were commonly left behind. I found yellowed copies of the Los Angeles newspapers, an old and much prized pocket watch, a gas lantern, and once the brightest jewel of all—a glossy copy of Playboy.

The trains were a thrill even at night and at home. I kept my door closed and the window next to my bed open. Its screen kept out most mosquitoes and allowed in the delectable sounds of night, most especially the distant, bracing whistle of an approaching freight train. A massive rumble and groan swelled as the train got closer. Meanwhile, the metallic ding-ding of the bell sounded from the crossing a block away. Then followed the low pitch of rumbling wheels as the caravan passed through. The melodious tee tawn tee tawn was a sedative. My thoughts decoupled as I lost count of passing boxcars.

Our neighborhood had a cast of transient characters. Mailman Jack in walking his route routinely read postcards before placing them into the curbside letter boxes. Sometimes he made exceptions. He started delivering Mrs. Barnes' mail to her door, even bringing it inside, after Mr. Barnes left her. She seemed to receive mail every day.

The Fuller Brush Man came knocking every few months. The Fuller Brush Company employed a legion of peddlers who hawked an assortment of brushes to American housewives. They were expected to walk six miles a day in attending to their routes. Their most famous agent was an evangelist named Billy Graham, though he never called on the Levines. Before he became famous, and then infamous, Pee Wee Herman went door to door for the company. Our representative was well dressed, a man of about forty.

He always wore the same double-breasted grey suit. A red sweater beneath his jacket hid most of his white dress shirt and his gray tie. He topped his balding head with a gray Stetson fedora. A thin ribbon secured a rust-colored feather that I always assumed to have once belonged to a pheasant. His black loafers were grass stained. One side of his brown leather brush case was scarred by his efforts to fend off the fangs of his natural nemeses, neighborhood dogs. Kathyren always let him in. We, or at least I, never learned his name. He was simply the Fuller Brush Man. Kathyren let him cross the threshold because she received a "Handy Brush" free each time she did. The sales pitch was always the same: "Mrs. Levine, today I got luxury hair brushes on sale. You gotta choice of boar bristle or horse hair. Both come with a five-year lifetime guarantee."

She accumulated plenty of Handy Brushes over time, but never once do I recall her buying anything from him. He ended his spiel by asking mom if there was anything around the house he could do for her. I saw him move a chair or two, nothing more. His closing was consistent.

"See you in a few months. By the way, do you know if Mrs. Barnes is home today?"

Jehovah's Witnesses came around. I had heard that they did not observe Christmas, Easter, or birthdays. Mother questioned my understanding, but I persuaded her to ask if the rumor were true. One afternoon, she greeted their knock on the front door. I hid behind a nearby chair to overhear the Witness's response. Mom did not ask them anything. She quoted part of an obscure Biblical passage and told them they were going to hell. The door slammed in their faces. They did not return for several months.

Avon ladies learned not to knock. Dad saw to that. Doorbells rang from coast to coast, but not at 2740 24th Avenue. For one thing, we had no doorbell. Nevertheless, they came. A woodpecker tap was followed by, "Avon calling."

"We're eatin' dinner, what the hell you want?"

"Is the lady of the house in?" came the tepid response.

"She's in the crapper."

Another rep would show up every so often and suffer the same abuse. The voices were always different. I never actually saw an Avon Lady.

The Good Humor Man visited the block every day during the summer. The Good Humor company began in the 1920s, and at its peak in the '50s, operated two thousand ice cream-dispensing trucks. The Good Humor Man was our Pied Piper. His off-tempo, recorded jingle cast a spell over us, drawing us to his truck like rats to their demise. The Good Humor Man dressed in white, with black shoes and a coin changer hanging from his belt. He wore a police-style cap with a Good Humor Wing attached. His selections forced most of us to make the first conscious decisions of our young lives. He carried eighty-five products, yet we typically had but a nickel to spend—a momentous decision indeed. There were Eskimo Pies and cream-filled orange sherbet bars, and popsicles among his wares. I chose popsicles because the sticks could be repurposed for school projects after their original duty was seen through. I wondered why drivers changed, thinking they most likely got fired for eating all their ice cream. That's what I would have done.

The shrieks and cries and general chaos of children were constant. Our house was the smallest on the block, but had that big, enticing yard. I'm convinced that my organizational skills dated from then, when I was the self-installed kid coordinator. At first, I knocked on doors to see who wanted to come over and play. My job got easier when we got our first telephone.

Houses in our neighborhood all were connected on party lines. As many as four families could be on a single party line at a time. Pacific Telephone discouraged long conversations, and they advised giving up the line in the event of an emergency. "My baby is sick," usually cleared the line for outgoing calls. I used my most serious twelve-year-old voice to announce yet another kiddy illness to assemble the next round of front-yard frolic. Our number, Gilbert 68705, was usually busy. When I was not organizing the gang, Kathyren often clandestinely sat in on conversations. She was a frequent listener. I once caught her penciling notes on a pad, the receiver off the hook. When I asked about her flagrant activity, she said she was practicing her spelling.

Mother, with all due respect, was a poor speller. I was worse. This became evident a couple weeks into one fall semester. I got nailed for playing hooky, having stayed home to listen to the World Series. Two days before, the Yankee's Don Larson had pitched a perfect game against Brooklyn's Dodgers. I was determined to cheer on the Dodgers in the seventh and final game. I handed my teacher an absence excuse the next day. The following morning found me seated across from the vice principal and the school's truant officer. My teacher had ratted me out!

"Who wrote this note, Charles?" I knew I was in trouble. No one called me Charles except when I was in trouble. There was only one thing to do—lie.

"My mother did, Mr. Woodall."

"Are you sure you are telling the truth, Charles? Cutting school can mean suspension, or time in juvenile hall."

"Yes I am, Officer Goldstone."

Woodall handed the penciled note to my mother, who had been listening from behind a partially opened door. It read: "Dear Miss. Ransom. Please xcuse my son Chuck for missing school yesterday Whensday October 10 1956. He caught the flew. Thank you Mrs. Levine." Somehow, they had caught on to me.

My Parents

M y father was an angry rattler, coiled to strike. He left behind the scars of venomous, often painful, childhood bites. He used a belt on me, and a hand on my mother. So it was that I harbored resentment against him, yet I felt pity more than anger. Dad memories are a mix of what I witnessed and of what Kathyren said about him.

Jacob Bernard Levine was born June 4, 1922, in Fort Worth. Dad—he went by Jack—moved to Los Angeles at about age fifteen and returned there after the divorce. I visited him occasionally before he died.

Jack's father, Ralph, was a Russian Jew who immigrated to Galveston from Polona in 1912. Attempts to trace the family tree have failed. Most records were lost, yet, Ralph's appearance told a story. In his late sixties, Grandpa resembled an alley cat, which had lost most of its fights. A "Caponian" scar marked his left cheek, and he was missing part of an ear. His battered grey face was drawn. His fringes of patchy hair were the color of nicotine and the burned cigarette paper that littered his raunchy room. The old tomcat was dispirited, and just like second–hand smoke, his unhappiness was lethal to everyone around him.

Ralph did not like his four children. Ralph only read Hebrew and spoke little English. He repeated the same sentences both times dad took me to his grungy downtown L.A. room: "Vat are you doink here? Vat da hell you did weeth my birth certificate?" Jack referred to his father as "the crazy old bastard." Watching them, I saw one common trait: They detested children.

Dad's appearance defied his conduct. His calm, aristocratic face disguised the turbulence boiling behind it. His clear light blue eyes never dilated; they looked like marbles frozen in their sockets.

His mouth was sensual but rarely allowed loving words. His lips were often pursed. Jack's nose was proud. Alopecia was winning the battle with his hair. He stooped when walking. He affected a stamp of superiority, but his cover was blown when he spoke.

Like agitating thunder from the forecast storm, Jack was aroused by the shortcomings of humankind as he perceived them. He often shouted derisively about other people and their ideas as he understood them. His uninformed speculations were an angry jumble of poor grammar and expletives. He saw himself as a martyr, victimized at the hands of his employer, his wife, the car dealer, and anyone else he regarded as wanting something, imagined or not, from him.

A psychologist named Lewis Engel once speculated that our unconscious desire to maintain family ties is so powerful that it can drive us to abandon our own aspirations and otherwise sacrifice the things we value most. Jack's approach to life defied that notion. He was devoted only to himself. His inability to get along with people marked him: He had no friends and seemingly substituted impractical dreams for that shortfall. Jack lived in a cloud of a thousand possibilities. He always had a half dozen projects in various stages of gestation, without a plan to implement even one. He was restless, but was at a loss as to how to convert that energy into success. He was "the un man." Most adjectives with an "un" prefix applied to Jack. He was unsuccessful, uncaring, unlucky—and, most obviously, unhappy. He was a man living in the wrong house.

Jack left when I was six. I felt abandoned. I had little contact with dad until adulthood. My attempts to connect with him went unanswered. At age nine, I wrote one letter, then backed off:

April 26, 1953

Dear Daddy
How are
you. I have a bike
now. Grandpa
fell off a hay.
truck " " and hert
his back. He coul-
dn't get out of a
chair " " for a few
weeks. He had
to sleep in it. he
had to eat in it.
He had a sling
on his arm. But
the last time we
went out their. He

was up and around. Mother said that I might be able to come up a few Months "this somer. I have ben geting a allowance" for a downpayment. Ever month I take all my allowance" out of my bank "" and give it to Mother" to help pay for my bike. Are you still working at a drugstore? I hope so. Mother let me have the desk" "so I can kep my cub scout things in it. If you dont no Mother works at the telephone co.. In to more months school will be out. The name ov my bike is a roadmaster. Where are you stay-ing at? All I nead on my bike" "is a batre for the light" "and a louch Wright me agian? Why dont you come up sometimes

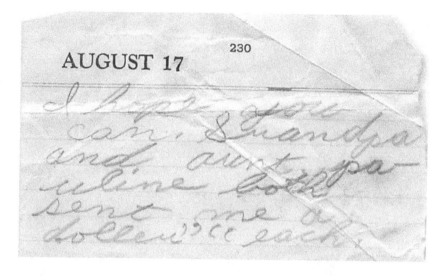

AUGUST 17

By exiting, Jack left behind his gifted little vocabulist. I was effected, yet did not get why. His surgical indifference to the needs of a son confused me. Like water, the unmarked element of dad's glaring disregard, found its low mark. We never were close after he left.

For years, I have wondered what attracted my parents to one another. My inquiries never received more than a muted explanation of how and where they first met. It was during the Second World War at Mather Air Force Base, outside of Sacramento. That's all I was ever told.

Jack claimed to have been an airplane mechanic in the army Air Corps, and he may have been, but watching him attempt home repairs left me with doubts. I came to believe that if he had been telling the truth than anything he laid a wrench to soon fell from the sky. Mom had difficulty describing her job during the war. I gathered she worked alongside Rosie the Riveter.

Jack was a human squirrel, though storing up cheap paperbacks rather than nuts. Books filled most of our living space. They were stacked in all three rooms, including the combination tool shed and bathroom. He owned a pair of reading glasses, yet I rarely saw him open a book. Education was not stressed in our home. Still, by sneaking peeks at his literary works, I received a cursory education in female anatomy. My guess was, and is, that Jack's stockpiled books, and a growing collection of first-issue stamps which ultimately proved worthless, gave him something he could hold on to.

All of this is to say that Jack was an ordinary, ineffectual man who spent more time dreaming about life than living it. He took us house hunting on Sundays, days that began infused with hope that gave way by noon, sunk by tension. I do not recall a single happy ending to any such Sunday excursion. We piled into our gray, 1940 Plymouth sedan. Kathyren sat next to him with me in the back. We drove around scouting about for Realtors' for sale signs. When Jack spotted one, he stopped and stared like a deer hunter with an eight-point stag in his sights.

"Everyone keep quiet, I'm thinking."

We sat for five or ten minutes awaiting his verdict.

"That one's the wrong color. Let's keep looking."

Three or more stops were made on a good Sunday, but we never got out of the car. Dad always said the same thing once we returned home:

"Well, did you enjoy the day? Go make me some dinner, Kathyren. I'm exhausted."

I failed to understand why we never looked into a bigger house. We certainly looked at plenty.

By evening, the two of them were yelling at one another in a remorseless cycle of rage. I often thought of running away.

I was no more than five or six and wondered if they actually liked each other. "And they lived happily ever after," was not to be the last line in my parents' tale. They divorced in 1950. Jack moved to Southern California, and we heard that within months he had hired on as a grocery clerk and had a new wife, lucky her.

Despite his limitations, despite his inability to master anything, least of all mathematics, he could multiply, fathering five girls in as many years with his new wife.

One day, years later, when I was married to Maura, I received a call from a nurse at Memorial Hospital in Santa Rosa, California: my mother was dead.

Hours before, while visiting Kathyren as she lay on what turned out to be her deathbed, I went to the hospital cafeteria for dinner. She was dying of cancer and a doctor candidly said she had just days remaining. I picked at a salad and nursed a glass of wine while summoning the courage to have a final, meaningful conversation. I returned to her room, 210, and sat beside her.

"Mom, we've had some wonderful times together. I know things haven't been easy for you, but you endured, and you've always supported me. I love you from the depths of my heart. And I know God does, as well."

She raised a weak hand and signaled me to move closer. I leaned forward and placed my ear near her mouth.

"You've been drinking," she whispered.

Those were her last words to me.

She turned her head to the side and fell asleep. I went home to do the same. I figured I try again tomorrow, but the nurse's call as I lay beside my wife ended that ambition.

Kathyren Mary Froehlich Levine was a dedicated, loving mother, who lived a hard life. She was born on October 17, 1916, several years too early. She seemed dumbfounded by anything that was plugged into a wall or motor driven. Most disturbingly, Jack had destroyed her faith in people. For that reason in part, she never remarried. I was the one bright spot in her otherwise dismal life.

Her English was woeful, and I never learned her native German. When I asked for help with my homework as a child, she said, 'look it up in the dictionary,' even if my request dealt with math or science. She was convinced all knowledge resided in the dictionary, although we never had one at home. Still, Kathyren was a good woman who despite little to live for, carried on, mostly for my sake, I figured.

My mother's early life read as a sequel to Hansel and Gretel. Kathyren Mary Froehlich was the second child of a poor German farmer name John, who married a witch-like stepmother, shortly after the death of his first wife.

Sometime during 1915, John and Bruna settled outside Bismarck, North Dakota, having immigrated from Kisel, Russia. Kathyren was one of five children born after their arrival, and Bruna died during giving birth to the last of them. Shortly afterward, John remarried Freida to help raise the children, who were pulled from school to work the farm. Freida, it was whispered, abused the children, spanking them and locking them in "the dark closet for the least of sins." Within a year, Freida died from an undetermined condition. Kathyren's sister Pauline became the family matriarch at age eight.

When she turned fifteen, Pauline married Herbert Tschoepe, another German immigrant. The twenty-eight-year-old farmer soon moved with his young wife to Point Pleasant, California, a tiny German-American enclave twenty or so miles south of Sacramento off Highway 99. In the 1940s, the community comprised a few homes, a general store, a church — the Evangelical United Brethren Church — and its adjacent cemetery, which had a larger population than did the settlement, full of late Schmidts and Schneiders and the like. Herbert and Pauline, like Hansel and Gretel, left crumbs along the way for their family to follow them. They touted the countryside and its Old World charms. Farmland was inexpensive, and everyone spoke German. Within a few years, Kathyren and my eventual uncles, Johnny, Leon and Walter, followed, Grandpa John in tow.

Point Pleasant, seen through the eyes of a seven-year-old Sacramento city slicker, was cows and pigs and bales of hay — and scary adults who spoke an indecipherable language. Kathyren and I spent the occasional weekend there. Holidays were a big deal. I enjoyed my seven cousins, although I was leery about the rural German-inflected, farming culture.

It was outside Point Pleasant that I witnessed a holocaust when I was six. Grandpa Froehlich took me to a slaughterhouse in nearby Elk Grove, where panicked cattle bellowed the certainty of their worst fear as they were moved along into the bowels of the abattoir. They were trapped between parallel fences leading to the executioners, who dispatched them with sledgehammer blows to the head. The Tschoepes had a hutch full of bunnies, and I named one I was fond of, not knowing that we soon would eat plump little Percy. I was introduced to plowing and cleaning out cow pens, learning nothing so much as that farming wasn't in my future. But Uncle Herbert strove to convince me, teaching me at five a.m. to pull milk from heifers' teats, advising me that that distasteful task would come in handy for me one day.

And, too, I helped Uncle Johnny with his pre-dawn Crystal Creamery milk route. That I enjoyed, riding high in the passenger seat of his big truck.

Other farm routines proved as unappealing as milking cows. Point Pleasant's red cabbage and sauerkraut did not match up to Good Humor's popsicles. And I was mystified by the Evangelical religion, which touted thrift, preached abstinence, and, while welcoming locals, shunned outsiders. The language was worst of all. At first, I thought German was sprechen to shield children from adult conversation.

The family had gathered for Easter dinner at the Tschoepes' home, fifteen relatives seated around a big table. Scary Uncle Herbert sat across from me. He clutched a knife in his right hand and peered down at me. He said something and looked at me expectantly. When he spoke, his large nose and heavy jowls moved in unison with his bobbing, black-rimmed glasses. I didn't understand a word, so I said nothing in reply. He tapped his thick index and middle fingers on the table, then barked at me, a stream of words of which only one—dummkopf—I understood. Then he reached for the butter.

BUSINESS ONE OH! ONE

Having advanced a bit up the Cub Scout ranks, I set my sights on becoming a Wolf. As a result, I got my first lesson in business management. I was in the second grade. There were six other boys in my den. Den Three was one of several in our pack. In scouting, as in the military, power came with rank.

As a Bobcat—the Cub Scout equivalent of a buck private—I found the going easy. I memorized the Cub Scout Oath and the Law of the Pack. Pack achievements involved knowledge of the Stars and Stripes, the value of religious rigor, physical conditioning, and the like. Sales were not mentioned.

We met weekly at our den leader's home, one Mr. Joe Paragallo. His son, Joey Jr., was in my den. The pack met every fourth Thursday. I had fulfilled all but one of the requirements to earn my Wolf Badge. Some of the boys built model airplanes to fulfill the last step. Others took credit for cookies their mother had baked. Mr. Paragallo tried to help out, suggesting I learn to tie complicated knots. None appealed, though something I learned at a pack meeting piqued my interest.

The pack leader announced a contest, pitting scout against scout, with the winners to receive awards. There were some fifty cubs in our pack. The way I saw it, not only was this a chance to win a prize, but to fulfill my final requirement to advance to Wolf. We were to sell tins of salve, door to door.

Each scout was given twelve tins at the end of the meeting. Profits were to help finance a field trip. I pulled a tin from the box when I got home. It was two inches in diameter and half an inch thick and the lid had an art nouveau motif on the rim with a green four-leaf clover in the center. It still does today.

The label read WHITE CLOVERINE. The salve, which the label made clear was registered with the U.S. Patent Office, consisted of "rectified oil, turpentine, white petroleum and white refined wax." It was, the label also made clear, "discovered by a physician."

Each one-ounce tin retailed for a quarter.

Kathyren pressed my blue, scout shirt the next evening. I slipped the triangular neckerchief around my neck, and captured its rolled ends in the brass neckerchief slide. On went my navy blue cap. I felt dapper and hit the neighborhood after dinner. This was the first shot at merchandising. I filled out a receipt for each sale. The first dozen tins sold fast. Within two hours, I was knocking on Mr. Paragallo's front door. I needed more salve.

"Hi, Chuck," he said. "Joey's in bed."

"I'm here about the salve."

"Did you not get your case?"

"I sold out. I need another dozen."

"Are you kidding!"

"No. I'm scouting."

I sold out again that night. It became a semi-weekly routine. After two weeks, I persuaded Mr. Paragallo to give me two boxes, rather than one. He balked initially, worried that I would be carrying too much cash. Six dollars was a fair amount of money in the day.

I ventured well beyond Twenty-Fourth Avenue, one door at a time. The next pack meeting was four weeks after the contest began. I was the market leader, having sold ninety-four cans of salve. Billy Tiedeman was second at the time, having sold but twenty-six. I had found my calling.

Sales increased as I polished my delivery. I replaced my original pitch—something like "Hello. I'm Chuck. Do you wanna buy a can of Cloverine Salve?"—with "Good evening, I'm Bear Cub Chuck from Den Three, Pack Two, of the Cub Scouts of America."

"Isn't that cute?" Or "How are you?" followed.

"I'm well," which I had been told was a better response than "I'm good." "Do you know anyone who might be suffering from chapped lips or minor burns? This would be a good gift for them."

I'm not sure if customers bought the salve for medicinal needs or because they found my pitch cute. It didn't matter. My closing ratio increased. I peddled seven cases the final two weeks. The night before the awards presentation, three tins remained. To insure my victory, I bought them with my saved lunch money.

The pack meeting was the big one, the year-end finale. I compared it to Little League Awards night, but not as elaborate, plus I was in better spirits, being in the game, and I expected to win. Picnic tables with blue-and-gold, paper tablecloths stood on the parquet floors. Nearly fifty scouts and members of their families were on hand. Dens were seated together beneath their banners. Our pack leader, Mr. William Tiderman, walked on stage. An American flag hung from a stanchion to his right, California's banner on his left. He called the meeting to order.

Chairs scraped across the hardwood as people stood. Tiderman recited "The Pledge of Allegiance" and offered up a pre-dinner prayer. Attendance was taken. Welcoming statements were delivered. Volunteers and parents were thanked for their help. Speakers reiterated the importance of scouting, while the aroma of hot dogs and burgers made us restless. I was sure I was not only going to win the prize, I was going to be awarded my Wolf Badge, and I asked Kathyren if she would have time to sew it on when we got home. She said she was proud of me and of course she would.

The last order of business was the awards presentation. Merit badges were distributed to several scouts, and den leaders received ribbons for jobs well done. Finally, Mr. Tiderman got to the contest.

"Our special thanks to Wilson Chemical Company for their valuable contributions to The Cub Scouts of America. Profits from their great product will be used to fund our field trip to Sutter's Mill in Gold Rush Country. Eight-hundred-thirty-four tins of White Cloverine Salve were sold by working scouts, with underlying support of their den leaders."

The room broke into prolonged applause.

"Tonight we are going to hand out prizes to the top three producers."

I did the math. Eight hundred thirty four tins divided by forty-seven scouts worked out to just fewer than eighteen tins apiece on average. I was the sure winner! I felt my heart throb in my ears. I began to wonder about the top prize; how would those pavement-pounding, cold, outdoor, November nights pay off?

Third place was announced first.

"I'm proud to say third place goes to Bill Tiderman, my hardworking son. Bill sold thirty-seven cans of Wilson's best."

Bill was given two movie tickets to see The Gunfighter, starring Gregory Peck, and a Swiss Army Knife.

Then it was time to reward the runner-up.

"Chuck Levine, please come up to the stage. Chuck sold two hundred twenty-eight cans of salve!"

I froze in my chair. What the hell? I looked at mom. She had reluctantly assented to the nightly salve runs. Her only child went off into the dark every evening for two months in search of something she didn't quite understand. I couldn't have cared less that more than one hundred people were clapping on my behalf. I barely remember taking the stage. I do remember I wasn't smiling.

Tiderman gave me the two-finger Cub Scout salute and said: "Good work, Bear Cub Chuck."

I felt like giving him the one-finger Chuck salute—not a good idea for an eight-year-old accepting an award, so restrained myself. I, too, received two movie tickets to see The Gunfighter, starring Gregory Peck, and a hatchet. Who the hell chose this prize? I expected a trip somewhere, and my Wolf Badge. What was I going to do with a hatchet? I walked back to my seat dejected.

"And now, the first-prize winner of our Cloverine Salve contest. The winner is Joey Peragallo. Joey sold two hundred forty cans of salve! Congratulations. Come up here and receive your award."

Joey looked dumbfounded. His dad seized his hand and pulled him to the stage. Joey received an expense-paid weekend for two to Lake Tahoe—and his Wolf Badge.

How the hell did Joey beat me? He was in bed by eight p.m. He wasn't allowed out after dark. That's when the action happened. Dads were home from work and moms were done with the dishes. Joey and I lived on the same block. I had visited every house within a half mile. I never once heard, "Joey already sold me salve," or "Joey has already been here."

I didn't sleep well that night. I knew somehow the contest had been rigged. I toggled back and forth between dejection and hope. They said I lost. I wasn't convinced. I had to find out what happened. Emotions were secondary. I didn't have enough life experience to leap to conclusion, but I could ponder. I feel asleep counting Joey's relatives and friends. He had about six of each, a number well short of the total tins he got credit for. I awoke with a start during the night.

My sleeping brain had stumbled on the truth: Joey hadn't sold the salve, his dad had! This guy made Uncle Herbert look like a saint. Mr. Paragallo, a k a Joey Sr., worked as a foreman at Bercut Richards Cannery in North Sacramento. I wasn't sure how many employees he managed, but I figured it had to be at least two hundred and forty.

That was my first lesson in Business One Oh! One. Eight-year-old Chuck realized that to get ahead, you had two choices: Either hire people to work for you, or have a sleazy dad.

I reviewed the Cub Scout credo the next afternoon: "On my honor, I will do my best, to do my duty to God and my country and to obey the Scout Law; To help other people at all times; To keep myself physically strong, mentally awake and morally straight."

I recorded the text and my scouting resignation in my best printing on a yellow, lined, eight-and-a-half by eleven sheet of paper. I dropped it, the movie tickets, and the last three salve tins in the Paragallo mailbox after dark. I kept the hatchet.

All said, I learned a valuable lesson. Uncle Herbert and Joey's dad both were important in my development. Their actions helped me better understand human behavior. The experiences armored me for future battles. I realized that control trumped subservience. I obsessed over getting tasks done quickly and correctly. These traits were often detrimental in youth. I lacked experience as a child. Consequently, I did things quickly and incorrectly. But I learned. I questioned Herbert's old-world treatment of children. Joey Senior needed to review his ethics. Both men had shortcomings, but I forgave them. I came away hurt, yet wiser from the experiences. At age eight, I had learned—thanks to Jack, as well—that the world was an imperfect place.

TELEVISION

As a child, I imagined the lambent outside world as visible, yet out of reach. My parents showed little interest in venturing much beyond Twenty-fourth Avenue—and at that only if absolutely necessary. There was no spark of originality or genuine creativity in my family, and little hope for a growing boy to discover himself and develop to his full capacity. I was curious, an explorer at heart. I wanted to escape. What I knew of the outside world came from reading magazines and listening to the radio. Kathyren and I spent evenings seated, facing the radio while eating TV dinners. And, then one day, through what seemed truly a miracle, my world leaped: We got a television. The Philco Company in the 1950s manufactured swivel televisions, which were notoriously unreliable. Ours boasted a twenty-one-inch, oval-shaped screen that turned on a Lazy Susan. When the set worked, it received the local stations of the three networks at the time: ABC, NBC and CBS. Reception was in black and white.

Naked City, a series inspired by the namesake 1948 motion picture, was my favorite weekly program. The narrator each week posed an existential question: "Do the machines of a factory ever need rest? Does a ship ever feel tired? Or is it the people who feel weary at night? There is a pulse to a city and it never stops beating."

Programs were filmed in magical, mystical, mystifying New York City. Episode plots typically emphasized criminals and their victims. The heroes battling the former and aiding the latter were, for the most part, mustachioed, tough detectives who perpetually smoked cigarettes like they owned shares in Phillip-Morris.

I was too young to sport a mustache, but I soon enough began smoking and wanted to move to New York. My affair with cigarettes was short-lived, but the series' iconic closing summation stimulated my lust for city life: "There are eight million stories in The Naked City. This has been one of them." Sacramento—often mocked as Sacratomato for the produce of its surrounding fields—was no longer the biggest city in my world. I was fourteen years old at the time and began contemplating a life in The Big Apple, all thanks to the magic of television. It would be years before I actually did find my way to The Naked City.

Baseball Hypothesis

For the next eight years I remained stranded in Sacramento, and it was there that my passion for baseball turned into ardor. I was a poor student, to the chagrin of teachers and professors alike. They became proficient at connecting the tips of reversed Cs, drawing a line from tip to tip to assign my grade. I didn't care; my future was in Major League Baseball. It was a pursuit I gave myself to year round, year after year. There was Little League from the time I was ten until I turned thirteen, then Babe Ruth League from the time I was fourteen to sixteen, and American Legion ball from sixteen to eighteen. I played in summer and winter city and county leagues, and on high school and college teams.

I did not, however, play baseball during my high school sophomore year. Poor grades kept me out of uniform. I got called from class in to the councilor's office for the bad news.

My academic counselor, Frank Ehrman, seemed angry when I entered his office. "Leave the door open," he said in a crisp counselor's voice. "Things don't look good, but I suppose you know that."

He sat behind a wooden teacher's desk, on top of which sat stacks of papers, a Remington typewriter, a 49er coffee mug, and a name plate that read:

Mr. Robert G. Ehrman III
Student Academic Advisor.

"Yes sir, I do." I said nervously, looking down at him.

Mr. Ehrman was a slight man, about five-foot six, and around 130 pounds. He was wearing a tan corduroy sport coat over a rumpled white shirt. A stained 'McClatchy' tie was knotted around his throat, and his hair was combed straight back. He glowered up at

49

me through glasses held together with Scotch Tape. A lecture was-coming, of that, I was certain.

"Well!" he said. "Charles, you are flunking out of school. Such a shame—you have leadership qualities, you are tall. You owe it to yourself to get good grades, to make a good impression."

"Did I upset anybody sir?"

"It's upsetting for a teacher to fail students. You've upset a few of them."

"Classwork's hard. I'm not interested in science, ain't got much need to study more English, and I don't like homework."

"You mean you're incapable of learning?"

"No," I replied. "I want to learn baseball strategy."

He took a deep breath and gave me a look. "I hate to see you left out Charles. But, we have an academic standard that must be met."

I tried to persuade him to downgrade the standard requisite from ineligibility to probation.

"I have a hypothesis,"

"Spell hypothesis," he said.

"I have a premise," I countered.

"Spell premise."

"I have a idea."

"Let's hear it, Charles."

"The Lions will battle for the Metropolitan League title if I play baseball. Ballooning attendance will increase concession sales. The school will sell more popcorn and hot dogs. Profits will increase if I'm allowed to play."

"Charles," he said. "McClatchy fields two football teams, three basketball squads, a track and field unit, and varsity and JV base-ball teams. One hundred and ninety boys participate in our athletic programs. You are the only one who is ineligible. Sorry," he added, "but I hope we don't have this conversation again next year. And, by the way, we don't have a concession booth."

And so, the lecture ended.

I was devastated. Yet, I owed Mr. Ehrman Three for having done his job. Thanks to him, my failure led to success. I stopped repeating the same ignorance-driven pattern that kept me off the diamond, and improved academically the next two years. The

Lions were in title contention both years—until about the sixth games of the twelve game-long seasons.

Not long after high school my baseball world continued to expand. I competed up and down the West Coast, at an advanced level of competition. One summer, I was named to a college All-Star team—the Grand Junction Eagles—and we played in Alaska, the exotic Far North. I had the privilege of playing with and against future major leaguers Larry Bowa, a shortstop and future major league all star. And there was the pitcher Kenny Forsch, who went on to star for the Houston Astros. Both were my teammates at Sacramento City College in the mid '60s. At City College, we had a stalwart rival in Fresno City College, which featured the future Hall of Famer Tom Seaver, who, one glorious day, we sent to defeat. I was the winning pitcher in that nine-to-three victory. I was well on my way; the transition from amateur to professional ball would prove seamless, of that I was certain. My talent was better than average—Hey, I bested the great Tom Seaver, didn't I?—but as it turned out, better than most wasn't good enough. I played my last game in 1964, four years before I received the letter directing me to report to active duty in the U.S. Army. I went from being an idealist, whose dream was to one day become a star professional baseball player, to being an unknown soldier.

HELLO GERMANY

While I wasn't good enough to join Seaver and Bowa and Forsch in the bigs, I was good enough—perhaps through the grace of the cosmos—that the US Army saw fit to ship me not to the hell and heat of Vietnam but to Mannheim, Germany, where General George S. Patton, not a quarter-century before, had died and the pheasants he sought to kill lived on. The World War II hero, while in route to the killing fields of rural Germany—where pheasants teemed and Patton sought to pursue them with all the fervor with which he had pursued Nazis—collided with, of all things, a military truck. Twelve days later, he died of spinal injuries. So it was that Patton's military life ended where mine began.

Mannheim is an industrial city in southwestern Germany, positioned at the confluence of the Rhine and Necker rivers in the state of Baden Wurttenberg. That region—the Rhine Rift—is Germany's warmest; summer temperatures occasionally hit ninety-five degrees Fahrenheit. In 1968, it was home to some three hundred and five thousand people, not including the visiting Yankees under arms. Mannheim was established in 766, its streets laid out in a grid—hence its namesake of Die Quadratestadt, or the City of Squares. In the city center, the streets have no names and are known instead by a combination of letters and numbers, such as C1 or L5. That's a blessing to foreigners, who are thus spared memorizing polysyllabic, German street names, such as some of the city's noteworthy citizens, like Baron von Drais Karls Sauebronn, who is credited with inventing the bicycle, typewriter and first meat cleaver, and Karl Friedrich Michael Vallant Benz, who in 1886 built the first automobile.

From June 1968 until I was discharged in late 1969, as it turned out, I lived in a former World War II concentration camp that had been converted into a U.S. military base. During the Third Reich, at least two thousand two hundred and sixty two of Mannheim's Jews were sent off to be exterminated as part of the Final Solution, Of course, the true final solution was for a defeated Adolf Hitler to put a bullet in his own head. During the war, Allied air raids almost completely destroyed Mannheim, which, at the time, was a critical industrial center for the Nazi war machine. In the 1940s, there were no such things as precision munitions—so-called smart bombs—rather the tens of thousands of pounds of munitions that fell on the city, and elsewhere, were indiscriminate. Mannheim's factories were destroyed along with most of the rest of the city as fleets of bombers of Britain's Royal Air Force and the U.S. Army Air Corps obliterated it, night after awful night.

I had no idea what to expect when I arrived in Mannheim, by then all but completely rebuilt. I wasn't an innocent by any means, nor was I worldly by any definition. Regardless, I had always prided myself on being quick to size up a situation. I wasn't bursting with self-confidence, but I knew how to survive. My first test to that end came just sixteen hours after my fellow soldiers and I reached our destination. We had flown from Travis Air Force Base to Rhein-Main Air Base, a U.S. Air Force Base near Frankfurt. Rhein-Main was the primary airlift and passenger hub for United States forces in Europe until the base closed in 2005. There, we were loaded into a Lockheed C-69, a silver plane with a dolphin-nosed fuselage and a triple tail assemblage. Passenger seats were installed backward and so we faced toward the rear in the opposite direction of travel. The prop engines' loud, insistent thrum made conversation all but impossible. The man next to me slept. I felt alone.

My thoughts, like the seat I was strapped into, looked back. I thought back to Terry Nelson, a classmate at Sacramento's C.K. McClatchy High School, named for the publishing mogul. Terry was the first person I knew who died in Vietnam. He hadn't been interested in college, and enjoyed working on his red convertible, a '55 Chevy Bel Air. It was a beauty. Terry was destined to take over his father's gas station, Mack's Mobil on the corner of Franklin Blvd. and Atlas Ave., just as soon as he returned home from his stint in the army.

I worked summers at Mack's Mobil, pumping gas, washing windshields, checking under the hood and repairing tires alongside Terry. Although he was more reserved than most of my friends, we got to know each other pretty well. I enjoyed his company in part because he laughed at my jokes, even the bad ones, which were most of them. Somehow he reminded me of Tom Sawyer. Terry had a copper-colored crew cut and a freckled face and one green eye and one brown, which lit up when he laughed. I told him he looked like a tilted pin-ball machine just to make him laugh even harder. Then one day, my memories of him irrevocably changed. Terry was killed in 1967 in a UH-1 Huey helicopter crash in South Vietnam. I was working with Mack when word arrived. "No!" he cried, and dropped to his knees. The formal uniform-clad messenger laid an envelope containing Terry's paperwork on the Bel Air's trunk, did an about face and walked away. It was the first time I had seen a man cry.

That's what I thought about during the clamoring flight.

I also reflected on the fact that the surname of Levine in the country where I was fated to serve had been a death sentence. I wondered if the prejudice against people with names like Goldstein and Rosenberg and Cohen—and Levine—had lived on after Hitler had died. In my own German-rooted family, discrimination existed. Point Pleasanters, for certain, disliked black people. They never forgave Kathyren for marrying a Jew. Now I was assigned to duty in the very nation where the Holocaust had been conceived. Moreover, I didn't speak the language and I had little money. Eventually, the travel caught up to me and I fell asleep, only jarred awake when the landing gear descended, locking the plane's wheels in place. It was one a.m.—the tail end of the witching hour—when we arrived at our new "home." It was a Sunday and I assumed there would be services I wouldn't attend.

Two buses met us on the tarmac, belching black, diesel smoke. We gathered our duffel bags, deplaned and climbed aboard the buses as yellow as the ones that carried children to class. We were bound for Bad Kreuznach, where we would be processed and assigned to our units.

I sat several rows behind the driver. A private from Texas took the seat next to mine, dumping his duffle bag on top of mine—both identical—before reaching down and unzipping a side pocket. He removed a Bible and a Superman comic book. A book marker marked his place in the comic book, unlike the Bible, from which nothing protruded. He was in his teens, clear eyed, well groomed, and sat up straight. Then he spoke.

"Howdy, partner. I'm Too Tall."

"I'm Charles." I had abandoned Chuck, the name I had chosen to appear on my eventual and inevitable baseball card.

"Where you from Too Tall?"

"Brownsville. Same as Janis Joplin," he said, though she actually had hailed from Port Arthur, Texas. "How 'bout you?"

"Northern California."

"Seek ye first the Kingdom of God and his righteousness and all these things shall be added unto you. Matthew: 6:33."

"And exactly where is that kingdom?" I stupidly asked, and looked out the window hoping that Too Tall would simply ignore my question.

"It's all around ya. It's in the sky, in the air, in the clouds, on the dirt, in this bus. It's everywhere."

"How tall are you, Too Tall?"

" 'Bout 6'4". Janis was 5'6" until she died, and that day she saw Jesus coming at her and He declared, 'Here is the Lamb of God who takes away the world.' John 1:29.9."

Too Tall believed the world was not our real home. Life on earth was a practice game in preparation for the next big event, a world of higher power commanded by God.

Too Tall and I were later assigned to the same unit, and I offered up a sincere prayer that I would be assigned to one end of the barracks and he to the other. Too Tall's hobbies were weight-lifting and fist fighting. He skipped breakfast mess, instead drawing sustenance from something he chewed on during reveille. This went on for months. Eventually, I found out he was eating his Bible. He had soaked the New Testament in LSD before leaving the States, and by then had worked his way through Matthew and Mark.

For now, we pulled out, westbound on Autobahn 60. The seventy-six-kilometer drive to Bad Kreuznach took an hour. Hardly a word was spoken. Heads lolled against windows and on their neighbors' shoulders until nudged off. Too Tall silently read The Adventures of Superman, his lips wagging along. German music drifted in and out from a gray transistor radio the driver had propped against the windshield. I took in the countryside.

What little I knew of Germany I had learned from newsreels and movies about the two World Wars. Accordingly, my views were biased. Just as books were printed in black and white, so, too, were my views. I hadn't considered that the sky over Germany was blue and the trees green, though I knew the spilled blood of Hitler's victims was red. So, as I peered out on that colorful June afternoon landscape, already I had learned something—what exactly, I wasn't sure.

We exited A60 and drove into a fourteenth-century painting. The asphalt highway had allowed a smooth bus ride. The previously unchallenged suspension now gave way to cobblestone. Everyone aboard woke up except Too Tall. Shouts of "Where the hell are we, slow this fucker down!" and the clicking of Zippo lighters didn't disturb him. He snored lightly with a half-grin on his face, and I presumed he was deep in a dream about Uberman. His left hand clutched his rolled-up comic book. His right lay in his crotch. I opened a window to suck the now choking smoke out. Church bells pealed. The village streets were narrow, and our bus slowed accordingly, pulling onto turnouts to let oncoming traffic pass, occasionally stopping. There were no sidewalks. Building fronts ended at the street. Duvets of all hues hung over open window sills. Uniformed passengers stared out at German citizens, the citizens stared back— a curious alien touch— both wondering what it would be like to be on the other side of the glass windows.

The driver blew his horn before each turn in the ancient road. I looked out on a Renaissance wall and at semicircular arches and columns, niches and hemispheric domes. I didn't own a camera, nor could I draw or paint, yet those images were recorded in my memory. I see them as clearly today as I did then.

One soldier bitched that American roads were better. Another griped that the driver needed to lay off the goddamn horn. I began to conclude that I had little or nothing in common with anyone I had so far met in the army. No better, maybe worse, definitely different. The Leadheads and the Too Talls dominated the milieu. I felt alone and insecure and wondered if my faculties would survive. I felt my frustration turning to anger.

We arrived in Bad Kreuznach in mid-afternoon, where a corporal met us at the bus stop. We shouldered our duffel bags and followed him along a gravel path that crunched beneath our army-issued boot soles. We arrived at a Quonset hut, one of many. I began to feel my privilege, earned on the fields of sporting battle, was being abused. Surely, Joltin' Joe DiMaggio, Whitey Ford and Ted Williams, the Splendid Splinter, would have been accorded better treatment—and where the hell were Seaver, Bowa, and Forsch? Yet, because I had failed to join the former bunch in the pantheon of baseball immortals—or the latter in the big leagues—Philly Chuck Levine swallowed his righteous anger. Yet, somehow, I had begun to believe in my sense of illusionary privilege.

An NCO sat at a desk near the entrance. He seemed too old to sport just three stripes. He was bald and wrinkled. Dark circles underscored his eyes like those of a man who had not slept in days. An electric fan at his feet circulated the scent of an alcoholic. The sergeant rifled through a file box, mumbled something and pulled out the one that matched the name on my shirt.

"You're joining the 7th Cav in Mannheim, La Vine. Congratulations. The bus is right outside that back door." He pointed in case I wasn't sure where it was. "You need to get on it."

He yawned and handed me the paperwork. I asked him if my spikes had arrived. He blinked a few extra times and began digging in the box again. "Don't see 'em here."

Two others had been assigned to the 7th Cavalry. A private named Paxton joined Too Tall and me on the army bus bound for Mannheim. It had been the longest two days of my life, and it wasn't over. California was five thousand and eight hundred miles behind me. I took a seat in the back of the bus, thankfully alone, and stretched out for the hour-long ride. The engine turned over, and the smell of burning fuel filled the air. I closed the window. Twilight had fallen.

The bus circled a roundabout and passed a park with willow trees and a lily-blanketed pond. Nearby, a woman sitting there shaded her eyes from the fading sun with a red parasol. A breeze picked up and scattered leaves on the path in front of her. Ducks rose from the water and flew off. This was a setting awaiting Haeselich's brush.

My effort to avoid the horrors of Vietnam had succeeded, but I had failed: I wasn't supposed to be in the army; I was best equipped for civilian life. The 7th Cav, I soon found, trained other soldiers for jungle warfare. That struck me as odd: Where were jungles in Germany?

Nightfall had arrived, and the headlights of passing cars passed through the bus, front to rear. Paxton I could see across the aisle and a few rows ahead was writing what I took to be a letter. Too Tall was out cold on the aisle floor. Jungles in Germany? My visions of an eight-to-five workday dedicated to baseball and Huck Finn adventures on the Rhine dimmed. I was concerned about what lay ahead. The real world was becoming abstract, or the other way around.

My war with the army had begun. I had been in Germany eight hours and already knew I was an outlier. I understood army speak, but did not speak it myself. Perhaps because I didn't have the amplified bark that delivered it in alpha commands that spoke of an earlier stage in evolution, an idiot's volume to cow the lesser apes: "Attention!" "Hut two-three-four!" "About face!" and the boisterous like. I was wired to resist. The demands made of me—and of my fellow grunts—made as much sense as an infielder chasing foul balls sailing deep into the seats. I felt that my head rested on a block merely awaiting the liberating fall of an invisible ax—a shrink, or perhaps a friend, presumably one not named Leadhead or Too Tall.

The trip ended at the gates of the Coleman Army Barracks, twelve kilometers outside Mannheim. In 1944, my birth year, the SS held POWs there from Poland, Luxembourg and Russia. After World War II, the United States Army took over the barracks. In 1951, Coleman Barracks served as the staging area for all troops arriving in Germany. Rumors circulated of an extensive set of tunnels beneath the base, the tunnels and underground facilities supposedly flooded after the war. There were reports of an alley that ran behind a particular cluster of barracks, where lay numerous bunker entrances, all of which were rumored to be sealed. These rumors persisted over the years and stories of hidden Nazi bunkers and underground tunnels were passed on from one generation of soldiers stationed at Coleman to the next.

The bus had stopped between two guard shacks. An arched sign above spanned the gated entrance. Its shape brought to mind Reno's colorful greeting, "BIGGEST LITTLE CITY IN THE WORLD." Its words read "COLEMAN BARRACKS US ARMY" in black and white did not project the same welcome.

An eight-foot, chain-link fence, topped with concertina wire, disappeared into the night on either side of the guardhouses. Searchlights above swiveled the depth and width of the base's perimeter. The road continued on several hundred feet past the gate. Toast-colored, hotel-shaped barracks on both sides funneled to a vanishing point in the middle. The street was deserted. Was this place meant to keep people out or in? It was now eight o'clock on Sunday night. Where was everybody?

I wasn't the only one asking the question. My fellow soldiers—and for the moment I did feel a certain camaraderie—thought it out loud. Paxton was hungry and expressed his concern that he would go unfed. Too Tall wondered aloud where he could get laid. The guard seemed understanding, winked, and waved us on. We drove by a row of prosaic buildings and were dropped at Company Headquarters; the bus then continued on. Our arrival woke the Spec-4 on duty. He was put out.

"You're late, goddammit. Why you late?"

No one answered. I considered the rabbit's line from Alice in Wonderland, but I held my tongue. The corporal walked us next door to our housing block. He took our paperwork and told us to report in again in the morning.

Our barrack was a dormitory, twenty men housed on the first floor and twenty on the second. Metal beds were positioned opposite one another in equal rows perpendicular to the long walls.

Green, black-numbered lockers stood along the walls between the beds. A footlocker sat in front of each. Too Tall headed upstairs, and I took my cue and found an empty bunk downstairs. Paxton did the same.

Everything I had learned, or thought, about military discipline and order was turned upside down that night. There was disorder everywhere and in every manner. Only five or six of the twenty beds on our floor were made. A copy of Stars and Strips lay open atop a locker. Coloring books and crayon stubs lay around. Beer bottles cluttered the floor. Cigarette butts filled a green Maxwell House coffee can. The tell-tale smell of cannabis hung in the air. I peeked into the door-less john, where there were six toilets and a ten-stall shower. Water ran in one of the toilets, none of which offered any privacy. In the bunkroom, Jimi Hendrix sang "Hey Joe." Garbage was strewn about. Uniforms, additional comic books, and trash of various hues lay scattered like a Jackson Pollock-inspired collage. I thought perhaps they had inadvertently dropped us off at a particularly riotous frat house, albeit one with open dorms.

THE MISFIT IS ALOOSE

I emptied my duffel bag onto the bed I had claimed, an extra uniform, boots, underwear, dopp kit, a pair of civilian khakis, brown loafers, a red turtleneck shirt, cigarettes and half a dozen paperbacks. That was all I owned. Paxton had fallen asleep. I failed to disengage my brain from what I was seeing. Coleman Barracks was my new address. Home was an ocean away with no return. I needed a drink. I changed into my civvies and sought one out. Coleman Army Base occupied land enough to fit twelve golf courses. The walk cleared my head. I reasoned that if every soldier but the newbies were out, there had to be a bar somewhere around. Never mind that it was Sunday night. That seemed one benefit of not being in a land founded by Puritans. It was the first optimistic thought I had had in the past two days. The night was warm. Crickets chirped, seemingly oblivious to the fanning searchlights. Together, they were the only sensory distractions in the air. Fifteen minutes down the road, I approached half a dozen fatigue-clad Negro GIs standing directly in my path under a street light. They were boisterous and seemed drunk or at least stoned. One turned his attention to me.

"Hey sucker, where'd ya get that red faggot shirt?"

I ignored the question and asked where I could get a beer.

"Who let you on base, motherfucker?"

"I'm not looking for trouble, just a drink."

The night felt warmer. A searchlight for a moment lit us up.

"Keep out of our neighborhood, motherfucker," the only one who had spoken said, and added, helpfully, "The NCO Club is up the street." They made an opening to pass.

"Thanks."

Walking away, I felt a frisson of fear, but avoided looking back. No footsteps followed me, but still I left the road, favoring the darkness away from the street.

The bar wasn't fancy—just a small, square, block building with a few shaded windows and open door. Jimi Hendrix was playing there, too. Four steps led to the door. I walked in and was approached immediately by a uniformed staff sergeant who calmly asked for my ID.

I showed him my dog tags. He laughed.

"This is an NCO club. You're not allowed or wanted here. Beat it."

"Fair enough, but where can a future NCO get a beer?"

"I can't help you there, son."

The military's hierarchy prohibits interaction between the upper classes and the lower. In that caste system, I was, at present, an untouchable. Officers are at the top, noncommissioned officers in the middle, privates at the unenviable bottom. Officers can risk their futures for socializing with the lower castes. NCOs are allowed to befriend the privates, but most shun them to establish their firm hold on a rung above. So far, I had met two groups of brother warriors. Both considered me an untouchable.

What happened next was so strange that decades later I can't explain it.

The only way I knew back to the barracks was the route I came. It was now eleven p.m.—no time to seek shortcuts through this foreign neighborhood. I hoped my greeting committee had dispersed. No such luck.

"How'd it go, Sergeant Motherfucker?" the verbal one said, and grinned, his teeth white in the shadow of his face. "Now, whatcha gonna do, faggot?"

The others laughed. One blew his smoke in my face. I walked away, the threat seemingly left on the corner.

I had made it one hundred feet or so, all the while reflecting on the dual insults that had been hurled at me. I tried to shake them off—and failed. I snapped. I spotted a push broom leaning against a dumpster, snapped off its bristled head, and turned back. If I considered anything at all—and it's doubtful that I did—it would have been that not to retaliate would, eventually, bring more of the same.

I'm not sure the first guy—the one with the mouth—even saw me coming, but he definitely felt the crack of the broom handle across his nose. The blow knocked a plaintive yell from his lips and he fell to his knees. The wooden handle had cracked in two. I smacked another across his chest and he fell backward. The rest cursed and scattered. I carried the weapon from the scene of the crime as the loudmouth shouted, "Look what you did to me!" and he left it at that. I apparently was no longer a faggot or a motherfucker.

I felt my knees quiver and my breath shortened. I realized I could have killed one of them and that, had I, I most likely would be writing this from inside Leavenworth, the military prison west of Kansas City. None of the bunch had threatened me or made any move to harm me.

The ruckus drew seven or eight GIs out into the night. They spotted me with the abbreviated broom handle in hand and moved to surround me. I ran between two barracks into the adjacent row, gathered myself, and as quietly as I could entered a darkened barracks. I passed between two rows of bunks, careful not to prick the silence, and opened a door behind which steps led to a cellar. I crouched beneath the stairs, my heart thrumming. Somehow, something had led my pursuers to the very barracks where, if they descended the stairs, I was trapped. Their intrusion woke, it sounded like, half the soldiers above and amid curses and unveiled threats, the posse departed.

By now, with the immediate threat dispersed, I was perceptibly trembling, questioning my knowledge of myself. The unprovoked attack, mere minutes ago, would have seemed to me impossible; it wasn't in my nature. Yet, that's what I had done. I had intentionally injured two people with a deadly weapon, both innocent of any real wrongdoing. I had been in Mannheim now a matter of mere hours. The consequences of my crime might have kept me in the army's possession for years. I waited an hour or so and quietly returned to the ground floor, out the door, and made it back to my barracks. Sleep was out of the question.

LATER THAT NIGHT

The event, as I have come euphemistically to refer to that night, haunts me still, coming to mind now and then, often at inconvenient moments, as though to punish me for my punishable and shameful loss of control. I've remained aware ever since that tensions lie within that can defy control.

All of this had happened even before the rest of the platoon returned to the barracks. They began to drift in in small groups. They had been to Mannheim and clearly had found what I had unsuccessfully sought out. Some brought back beers and others turned on the radio. Soon, they were yelling over the blare of the radio and themselves. In the midst of the clamor, a cry came from the shower. I rose from my bunk to check it out. A cheering crowd had formed a semicircle around two men fighting. Too Tall had a GI pinned to the white tile floor on his stomach. He repeatedly banged the man's head against a toilet bowl. The soldier shouted a surrender, and they stood, their clothes covered in blood. Too Tall's nose was bloody and his lip split. The loser's eyes were all but closed, mere slits. He had lost a front tooth. And like that, it was over and seemingly forgotten. They shook hands and shared a beer. B Platoon had a new alpha dog. And I had a new home. Half a day of service completed, five hundred forty six and a half to go. Only thirteen thousand, one hundred sixteen hours remained. It was a depressing thought.

WHAT HIGHER BOND IS THERE THAN FRIENDSHIP?

I n the army, you could get away with being suspected of almost anything—other than a bent toward homosexuality. Ours was a chaotic society, where various subcultures came to often uneasy yet reliable terms. Group bias prevailed over individual rights, the latter of which no longer existed. Some rules were written, others tacit. Relations between those of varying ranks, ethnicities, religions, and physical strength could be negotiated. Homosexuality could not, and proof of such desires wasn't required. Suspicions were adducible in that court. Punishment was swift and brutal. Suspected gays were accorded blanket parties, in which the victim was restrained, a blanket thrown over his head, and the hell beat out of him. There were no appeals.

Racism, of course, didn't vanish with the swearing of an oath; rather, it induced others. Soldiers were stereotyped. Levine was a kike and so generally believed to have a good deal of money. I was regularly hit up for loans—I was, in fact, The First National Bank of Zero Assets—and even if I was sitting on half a fortune, it seemed a bad practice to finance debtors who had ready access to loaded weapons. Larger minority groups, predominantly African-Americans, Hispanics, and Italians—also known as niggers, spics, and guineas—transitioned into military life more easily than did smaller ethnic groups. Native-Americans, readily known throughout the ranks as nickel-less drunks, had a particularly tough go. The few in our unit had, in fact, enlisted to escape poverty. As new members of the 7th Cavalry—which had been General Custer's—they sacrificed ancestral pride for the sake of minimal financial gain. The switch from citizen to soldier presented challenges to all, but they suffered the most.

Most in our company, including non-commissioned officers, abused drugs, as well as alcohol. Marijuana, hashish, LSD, and methamphetamines were nearly as available as aspirin. The army, I soon learned, was a world of foggy escapism. Mix high testosterone levels, illicit drugs, and the virtual absence of women, and no match was required to set off a conflagration. Judging by how willing we were to fight ourselves, I figured enemy soldiers didn't stand a chance. Inter-company sporting events frequently ended in brawls. Paydays were guaranteed fight days. Frustrated soldiers vented off base. Americans fought German, French, and English soldiers inside and outside Mannheim bars. Otherwise, army life was workaday dull.

There was nothing to do between dinner and the sounding of taps other than to play cards, fight, listen to music, fight over that, and insult one another until one or the other had had enough and a fight was on. Two months into my military career, I started using drugs. Getting high offered relief—and then you came down. It was about then that I discovered why Too Tall was so enthusiastically eating his Bible. While often high—the heavy use of drugs did have the passive effect of cutting down on the fighting—I spent my evenings reading and writing letters. I also took a crack at writing a book: "World War Three in Germany Seen Through the Eyes of a Lovelorn Unhappy Californian." It was a lousy title and a worse book. It was conceived as an autobiography, and unless you expect to die at twenty six, there's no point in attempting such an exercise in hubris. As the stoned scribe, I realized within the first twenty-five pages of the first chapter, that I was no budding Norman Mailer and so I scrapped the month-long effort.

It was then that I met a fellow GI named David Cameron Craver, a "Gatsby-like guy," who as it turned out was literate and from New Jersey, in possession of all the things I wished for myself. Literacy alone was relatively rare among my fellow soldiers, and the army certainly didn't prize intellectualism unless, of course, that brainpower was directed at furthering the force's mission and ability to kill. David Craver wasn't so inclined. He had a real sense of the

Hippocratic Oath: Do no harm. His guiding principle was that all lives had equal value. Few other soldiers believed anything of the sort. Getting to know David was a lifeline that made my military life tolerable.

We met one Sunday morning in the Post Exchange. The PX was a large general store offering all manner of consumer goods and prepared foods, all at a discount. That morning, I was recovering from one of my frequent hangovers, nursing a cup of coffee. David was suffering from the same malady. We shared a booth.

David's posture certainly fit the military mold, back straight and shoulders squared. His brown hair was cut military short. His skin was bookishly pale. He wore wire-rimmed glasses. His eyelids drooped over light brown eyes. His nose was straight with a pointed tip. Lines at the corners of his mouth suggested a ready smile. His mannerisms suggested a man ten years older.

He scanned a recent copy of Stars and Stripes. I read the crudely carved inscriptions on the wooden table's top. I offered to swap publications. He laughed and we ordered another coffee. I offered him a smoke and we lit up. And so a friendship began.

We were close in age, but miles apart in status, military and civilian. We shared one ardent interest—getting out and back on with our lives. We were in the same company yet different platoons. He was a Headquarters clerk; I was an infantry scout. Otherwise, he came from affluence; I was poor. He played squash; I played baseball. He was born in New Jersey; I sprang from across the country. He was raised in a traditional family, with two parents and two siblings; My mother raised me alone. He had studied English at Trinity University; I went to Sacramento City College, then Cal State Los Angeles. He held a degree; I flunked out. It was only after sober, reflective consideration that years later I understood the effects of these polarities.

Our conversations were more than idle chatter—they helped us cope with the same banality and insanity that had inspired Joseph Heller to write Catch-22. David, too, opposed the war, yet reported for induction. He admitted he had been at least at the time burned out on academia. Despite, or perhaps because of, his

Milo Minderbinderesque circular logic, I cared about the opinion of another person in uniform.

He was deeply educated and knowledgeable and more than once I wondered in my insecurity if my constant questions—my quest to learn the sorts of things I may have if I had been at least a halfway competent scholar—annoyed him, if he found them off-putting. He was the sort who was utterly at home reciting excerpts from classical literature. David had read George Bernard Shaw, Oscar Wilde and Leo Tolstoy. The best I could say was that I had heard of them. I had come across them on college finals in classes that I had skipped. Now, removed from the pressure of test regurgitations, I began to enjoy reading what intellectual writers had written.

Who knew that my days and weeks and months in the United State Army would provide me an education I hadn't even realized I had missed and came to find I coveted. Reading became my nightly retreat while on guard duty and off. I enjoyed Donleavy's Ginger Man, Fitzgerald's Gatsby, and Guccione's Penthouse, but had difficulty with Poe's macabre tales. I pored over all I could find about New York City.

David and I often hung out after hours. There was nothing in the way of substantial entertainment at Coleman: censored B movies, foosball, and board games were pretty much it. We spent as much time away from the barracks as duty and pin money allowed. Mannheim had a flourishing red light district, largely catering to GIs. The city lay twelve klicks south of the base. A round trip on public transportation ate an hour. Frankfurt was an eighty-four kilometer train ride further on. Heidelberg became our favorite town. Local gasthauses proved largely affordable and definitely convenient. Such establishments became default destinations.

Leaving base with permission was all but impossible for me given my poor job performances. My incompetence cost me passes and leave. Illegally was another matter. One skill I had learned in basic training—and the only one I regularly availed myself of— proved useful: the belly crawl. Avoiding guards after dark was a simple matter. Soldiers cut body-sized openings through Coleman's chain-link fence faster than maintenance crews could patch them. After sunset, I'd lower my gut onto the ground and scoot along, slowly, like a slug approaching a leaf, across ten feet of no-man's land to the fence. Searchlights fanned by and I'd scoot through a cut in the fence, my shirt front and pant legs filthy, and meet up with David and a few other GIs who had become buddies. I never got caught.

THE ZANIES

G asthauses were combined inns and taverns that catered to soldiers. They also rented rooms. German girls were for rent, too. The inexpensive New Orleans Gasthaus was our favorite. It sat alone on the Viernheimer Weg, the two-lane road connecting Mannheim to Coleman. The two story Foursquare building looked like nothing so much as an American motel, nothing fancy. Warm beer was served in bottles, mixed drinks in scratched, red, plastic glasses. We drank beer, ate potato pancakes and schnitzel, and watched the goings-on; soldiers often became wildly irresponsible and only rarely got in trouble for doing so.

Patrons entered under an archway, which resembled Coleman's entry gate, into a dimly lit dining room. The bar ran the length of the right wall. A framed, faded forty-eight star, American flag hung above its shelved bottles. Women in revealing tops and short skirts perched along its length. Red couches with stained cushions fronted the bar. Candle-lit tables filled the rest of the room. The walls were sheathed in oak. Shades blocked out light; the place existed in eternal dusk. A hallway at the far end led past the bathroom to a door illuminated by a red, overhead light.

The hookers were not courtesans. Mannheim's red light district—Penisstrassen—attracted younger, more appealing girls. But New Orleans Gasthaus was not a brothel, it's just that it so happened to offer rooms for rent. The owners looked the other way, ignoring the so-called stool birds, because they brought in a goodly business.

Pretty much anything could happen at any time, particularly immediately after paydays. No different from many university frat houses, drinking contests, bottle throwing, and drunken fights were far from uncommon. With money to spend—savings were not a common consideration—GIs walked in, pockets bulging with marks, and stumbled out. In the interim, they courted action, however each man defined it. This was the first time away from home for many, and more than a few of them fell in love with the prostitutes. Courting—if it could be called that—was rote. A young buck chose a doe, or she picked him, and they adjourned to a couch. The GI ordered drinks and propositioned her. She needed another drink first. He complied and moved to the bar. The hooker dumped cocktail number one into the potted, rubber plant behind the couch. After two or more rounds, and the planter beginning to leak, the couple made their way down the hallway. At least, that was the case except for when the alcohol and dope proved too much even for the amorous soldier whose next liaison was with the floor. Buddies—or on occasion Military Police—hauled the GIs back to camp. The MPs'sobriety test was simple and all but impossible for the soberest of men: "Say 'mixed biscuits' fast, five times." No one passed. David and I occasionally took solace in the embrace of hookers, but otherwise ate dinner and spent an hour or two watching the action and knocking down a stein or four.

Afterward, we took a cab to within a few hundred feet of the camp. David, who never got in trouble and so never arrived at the gasthaus dusty from chest to toe, headed toward the main gate. I vanished into the dark in search of a fence cut.

The true oddities took place not in the gasthauses, but in the barracks. Private John Parlatore and Specialist John Stamps were, by most strict measures, diagnostically sane. Both, apparently, had passed the IQ and rational behavior portions of their military qualification exams. Yet, by observing their conduct, one could fault the validity of such testing. Parlatore liked to burn himself. Stamps ate light bulbs.

Parlatore was a muscle-bound private from Boston and the strongest man on post. No one messed with Big John. Not even Too Tall dared take him on. His Popeye forearms were scarred from cigarette burns resulting from a "game" known as hot sandwich in which a lit cigarette was laid between two opponents' bare forearms. Who ever yielded first, lost. A tie took some eight to ten minutes before the butt burned itself out. Somehow or another, the stench of cigarette smoke and burning flesh triggered excitement in the barracks. Parlatore was much admired for his acceptance of pain; his victory stripes bore evidence of that.

Stamps was a short, obese, mess-hall cook, who died just weeks before his retirement date arrived. Consuming light bulbs hadn't done him in; no, he was stabbed to death, the details of which I no longer recall. He had missed few meals in his twenty-year army career. When he wasn't eating his own cooking, he partook of incandescent light bulbs. I wasn't the only one that thought eating a bulb couldn't be any worse than eating his chow, but none of us ever ventured to find out. The effect of his obsession gave Stamps a certain odd stature within the company. He would pop a whole light bulb in his mouth, chew it, then wash down the smithereens with beer provided to him free by those who had urged him on.

Eleven months remained of my tour. Of course, there was one sure way for a soldier to put an end to his stay in Mannheim, but it required abysmally bad judgment. More than one soldier I knew opted for it. A levy, or shire levy was a means of military recruitment in medieval England. Shire levies were used to mobilize non-noble, able-bodied men, especially during the Hundred Years War with France. American levies were used in the same way, except as transfer orders for soldiers, especially during the Vietnam War.

Levies filtered down frequently from Bad Kreuznach. The assignments filled service openings created by combat casualties or by soldiers rotating home from Nam. Replacements came from within our ranks, transfers announced during roll call. No one understood the selection process. The first sergeant might have chosen names, or they might have been randomly pulled from a hat. Levies were never announced in advance. Had they been, desertion rates might have increased.

I was training as a long range reconnaissance platoon scout when I witnessed my first levy. A scout's survival odds in Vietnam at the time—1968 was during the height of the war—were low. Some died within seconds after first making enemy contact. So it was that I began to demonstrate an even worse military proficiency. I had decided never to become skillful enough at any job, let alone that of a platoon scout, to fill a vacancy in Vietnam.

David and I one morning stood before a levy call just a few months after meeting. All told, four platoons, about one hundred and sixty men, lined up in ranks of ten. July's sun rose in our faces. We relaxed at ease on the warming asphalt, unaware of what was coming.

Sgt. Maj. James arrived in his jeep, stepped out, and positioned himself before the company. The sergeant major was a ruddy, tobacco-chewing, fifty-something-year-old veteran, a lifer who looked the part, hardened by regimentation and violence. A frankness shrouded him, and he seemed incapable of any expression other than a frown. James quietly faced the group for a minute, surveying the company through sunglasses. Next to him was his driver, Parlatore, who had been promoted from the motor pool. He raised his bullhorn, took a breath, and said something along these lines:

"Good morning. The cavalry needs a little help stopping Charlie (The North Vietnamese Army). We've got six positions to fill this morning: two machine gunners, three recon scouts, and a radio operator. Are there any volunteers among you before I call out names? Those of you who volunteer, or extend your enlistment, will receive promotions and pay increases." The Sgt. Maj. abruptly dropped his arm to his side and spat on the ground.

Many GIs voluntarily rotated to "action-packed" Southeast Asia. The tendency was to glorify war as a place to become a hero. Young men often bought into the idea. Other distressed recruits, often those who had received a Dear John letter, volunteered resignedly.

More than six hands shot up that morning. Steven Glasspool, a private from my platoon, was among them. I whispered to him, asking if he figured his parents would prefer to bury him in a dark or light coffin. Down went his arm. He later thanked me. James congratulated the volunteers, did an about-face, and returned to his jeep.

The sad simplicity always moved me. A thin line between life and death was drawn by a few dollars and the raising of a callow man's hand. Half a dozen young men, boys really, had volunteered that morning to risk their lives for a pay raise and a second chevron. I tried not to dwell on their futures.

David and I met at the PX for coffee a few days later. We talked about how it was that we came to be in Mannheim. David's undergraduate degree was in English literature. He qualified for an officer's commission but was opposed to the war and so had turned it down. He was drafted soon after being offered a spot in officer training. He scored well on aptitude tests and was assigned to Fort Bliss, in New Mexico, where he trained as a Redeye missile man. The General Dynamics 43 Redeye was a man-portable surface-to-air missile system. It used infrared honing to track its target. In short, David's job was to shoot airplanes out of the sky from his shoulder. His parents evidently learned that systems designed to fire such projectiles led to high mortality rates. They somehow managed to get David reassigned to Mannheim. My next question—"How?"— was interrupted by Private Robert Medina, who had approached our table. He bummed a fag and asked if we preferred Triumph or BMW motorcycles. The question remained unanswered.

Medina, a loud eighteen-year-old, was proud of his Los Angeles roots, and of his ability to blow double smoke rings. He never paid for cigarettes. He normally packed a Risk board and played for cigarettes. Medina was one of the six recent levy volunteers. He had come to the PX to buy a bike with his re-up bonus.

The army encouraged dealers and shylocks to peddle their wares at the PX. Doing so increased enlistments. Re-up bonuses were taken for down payments. The chosen automobile or motorcycle awaited the GI upon his discharge. No collateral was required. The dealer kept the vehicle until the soldier finished his tour—if he did. Moreover, duties were waived if the buyer drove over six hundred miles before exporting the purchase to the U.S. Medina had opted for a BMW.

Medina was accelerating his army involvement. I was standing on the brakes of mine. He was combat-bound and soon to be promoted. As a Private E-2, almost everyone in uniform was my boss, and I was determinedly not upwardly mobile. Madina seemingly was fated for a trip to the hospital or to the morgue. I was doomed to fail because I engineered the impression that I was worthless.

The army mostly was filled with GIs unhappy from morning to night. We were wakened each day by a somber sergeant's shrill whistle. "Up and at em! Fall out! Get your lazy asses out of bed! It's morning!" I, along with most fellow soldiers, brushed my teeth, pissed, and hit on a joint, not necessarily in that order. Others started their mornings with a beer, or a page of scripture from Too Tall's New Testament. Brain-fogged, we dragged ourselves outside for the morning count. After roll call, I took another toke, and slunk off to underperform my day's work. The dope dulled me to the point that army life looked like something possible in the real world, like a game of pretend, with Coleman at the hub of the fantasy.

Between the narcotic escapes came daily duty, where I worked diligently to seem incapable of any shred of proficiency. As a result, I was often confined to base. I escaped on my belly at least thirty nights in my thirteen months.

Heidelberg was the safest escape destination. There were no MP patrols and few GIs. Five-hundred-year-old Heidelberg University had been home to Karl Jaspers and Georg Hegel among other great thinkers. It was currently home to several thousand female students, all the reason for a young man to visit the stunningly romantic little city.

David and I both sought love. Finding it while stationed in Germany appeared unlikely. I was willing to settle for a discounted version, periodically at the expense of a woman's emotions. David, however, was not so far as I knew, a womanizer. His fantasy woman was Miss B. Fitzdare.

J.P. Donleavy created her in The Beastly Beatitudes of Balthazar. Miss Fitzdare was a smart, beautiful woman of means, and an equestrian. She was single but unavailable to her suitor, Balthazar. David identified with Balthazar, "who looked in vain for the one thing that always eluded him: true love." Donleavy wrote that "Balthazar was born … in a big white house of a mother blond and beautiful, and a father quiet and rich." David had been raised in a big white house with his English mother and banking executive father. When Balthazar's father dies, the son is shipped to an English boarding school. David also had attended a boarding school, Blair Academy. Balthazar enrolled in Trinity College in Dublin. David attended Trinity College in Connecticut. David seemed to me self-assured and confident with women. He found his Fitzdare one freezing winter night in a Heidelberg nightclub. I had met her first. Her name was Patrizia.

Along with two fellow soldiers, Dan Freeman and Dave Ryan, I had taken the train to Heidelberg. We had smoked hash and left base for a night of fun. David wasn't with us.

Freeman was a pin-thin doper, an artsy type from California. His quick and dry humor made him a platoon favorite, yet, he, too, had no business being in the Army. He was the soldier an enemy would be pleased to encounter. He was harmless—a nervous guy incapable of sitting still. He continually crossed and uncrossed his legs. He tapped his fingers to music only he heard if no other was audible. He was obsessed with his air guitar and his goal in life was to screw Janis Joplin. "Give me five minutes with her. We'd be in bed, like that." He snapped his fingers for emphasis.

Ryan was a headquarters clerk, whom I never trusted. All I knew about him was that he chain-smoked, picked his nose over dinner, and didn't like his wife. Ryan got married to avoid sleeping in the barracks with a group of strange men. Married soldiers and their families had separate quarters from the rest of us.

We got off at Bismarkplatz hard against the Neckar River. Snow fell as we walked the block to Shepard's Lounge at Haupstr 18. The cold, metal door handle stung my bare hand. The wind had picked up. We pushed into the room and warm air greeted us. We took a table near the bar as its former occupants stood to leave. A waitress named Hanna approached and took our order. She wore a black, puff-sleeved blouse above a leopard-spot skirt. She soon returned with steins of beer. Freeman, Ryan, and I pooled our money for an entrée.

Shepard's Lounge was decidedly not a soldier's bar. The typically austere bars that accommodated GIs rarely reflected a modicum of German culture and charm. Shepard's catered to locals and occasional tourists. It could best be described as a vegetarian's nightmare. Furs, feathers, and animals' decapitated heads looked down over the room: sheep, boar, deer and foxes. Downed ducks and pheasants had their place. Most were available on the menu. Patrons relaxed around oak tables, seated on faux leopard-skin chairs. I fit right in with my tan khakis and red turtleneck. Up-floor lighting flooded the walls, stretching animal shadows eerily to the ceiling. A fireplace crackled. "Ob-La-Di, Ob-La-Da" played in the background.

A couple of beers into the evening and fully warmed, Dan proposed a toast to Andy Warhol, who after he was shot that year claimed he had no idea whether he was dead or alive. That existential question began when on June 3 a hanger on in his famous Factory named Valerie Solanas fired the bullet that struck him. Warhol spent the next two months of his life in a New York hospital recuperating from surgeries to repair his damaged lungs, esophagus, spleen, liver, and stomach. His injuries were so severe that he wore a surgical corset the rest of his life. We clinked our ceramic steins and drank up.

Customers continued to file in. I looked up at a petite blonde standing before us. She was covered in melting snow. "I'm cold," she managed. A fourth chair at our table was open, and I invited her to join us. I ordered her a sherry.

Patrizia Giusippina Michele was twenty years old and from Spain. She was studying at Heidelberg University. She was exquisitely lovely. Her hair was long, her eyes dark and her upper lip formed a cupid's bow. The conversation shifted from Andy Warhol to Heidelberg history. Her accent was sensual, her voice vibrato.

A long evening at Shepard's was too expensive, so the four of us bundled up and moved next door to Chequers. Two fräuleins already there accepted Ryan's invitation to join us. An hour later, David wandered in from the cold. He pulled up a chair. The party continued until after midnight when we began to make our way back to Coleman. The sky had cleared. Freeman, Ryan, and I led the way through the fallen snow to the station platform. David and Patrizia followed a few yards behind. We dropped her at a cab stand and caught the last train to Mannheim.

The return to Mannheim was drunkenly boisterous. Freeman, Ryan, and I shared our appreciation of Patrizia. There was something distinctly fine about her. David didn't say a word. I had managed to secure a date with her for the following week. For once in my Army life, I was neither dwelling on the past, nor fretting the future; instead I had something to ground me in the firmness of now.

We reached the barracks around two a.m., a mere three hours before reveille. I slept well and dreamed of Patrizia.

The next morning, the first sergeant summoned me to his office. I had received an Article Fifteen of the Uniform Code of Military Justice, a non-judicial punishment akin to a contestable traffic ticket, a way for officers to resolve allegations of minor misconduct against a soldier without resorting to more severe forms of discipline.

I was about to feel the stab of the sergeant's verbal cutlery, "Levine you disobeyed a direct order." he said.

"What order, sergeant?"

"On Monday morning, at 0700 hours, I ordered you to get your hair cut. Did you obey my direct order, Levine?"

"I did not, Sergeant."

"No, you did not, Levine, and as a consequence you will forfeit seven days' pay and you are hereby restricted to the barracks for fourteen days. You also will pull night guard duty in the tank section by the motor pool. Any questions?"

"Could you make it a month's pay and wave the confinement, sergeant?"

"You're dismissed."

I decided to contest the Article Fifteen and demanded a court-martial. In my infatuated mind, it was better to risk severe punishment than to stand up Patrizia. Two days later I went to the commanding officer to argue my case. After thirty minutes, I was informed he was out and would be so until Friday.

"Are you willing to let a lieutenant hear your case in his absence, Pvt. Levine?" the desk corporal offered.

"Sure, yeah, okay."

I followed him into an adjacent office. Sitting behind the desk was goddamn Lt. Cole from the Oakland Induction Center.

His speech was clipped. "How ya hittin' em, Levine? You look like you need a haircut."

I saluted him, signed the Article Fifteen, saluted him again, did an about-face, and left.

Patrizia and I were to have met at Shepard's on Friday night. Without post phone privileges, I had no way of reaching her. I was at a loss, and then a thought occurred: I'd send an emissary to explain my circumstances. Ryan was married and Freeman was unreliable. That left David.

David visited me the following night during my confinement to the barracks. He agreed to help me out.

"I'll go, Charles, but I want you to know I liked her, too."

"Go for it," I said gallantly." By the way, for what it's worth, she mentioned something about a boyfriend in Spain."

In an odd sort of way I was relieved. Patrizia struck me as altogether perfect, an ultimately intimidating notion. I had been nervous in her presence, and I now assumed she must have picked up on that. I thought about the fact that she had hung back with David on our way to the depot. It dawned on me that Patrizia and David had more in common that she and I had. She was in her third year at Heidelberg University, and David's refinement far eclipsed mine. David could recite all one hundred and thirty two lines of T.S. Eliot's "Love Song of J. Alfred Prufrock" flawlessly. He was articulate and polished. I could recite the names of all eight players in the L.A. Dodgers starting lineup. I realized the fallacy of my fantasy.

David returned a few days later. He had a bounce in his step and a new confidence in his voice. I knew as certain as my longing that he had slept with Patrizia, a realization that imperiled our friendship: Was the pleasure of a tryst stronger than our bond?

I had fallen in love with Patrizia at first sight and had had her stolen away without so much as a kiss. I had memorized a quote after a previous failed romance: "The danger of love is that of loss, yet something can be gained too, since surviving the ordeal results in a more substantial, renewed self." What a crock of shit, I thought.

David dropped by. I lit a Tareyton and read my Article Fifteen aloud. I protested its absurdity. David agreed and said, wryly, "Cupid works in strange ways." Despite my angst, I managed a grin. I looked into his eyes but decided not to ask the next question, he was obviously taken with her. I had spent but a few hours with Patrizia. I was disappointed, and a little pissed but kept my thoughts to myself. I faced a bigger problem, continuing to survive the madness of military life.

MATTERS OF ADJUSTMENT

I once read that the secret of happiness and virtue is liking what you have to do. Had I had my way, I would have spent the next year living in a castle, sleeping with Raquel Welch—or Patrizia—receiving my doctorate from Harvard, eating lobster tails, and playing centerfield for the New York Yankees. But I didn't have my way. Instead, I lived in a barracks, slept alone in the proximity of thirty-nine other men, received an Article Fifteen, ate crappy food, and pulled guard duty. Forget the secret of happiness and virtue; it wasn't going to happen here, not for me. I had moved from an apartment of my own to a barracks full of cursing, belching, fighting, farting, impulse-prone men.

Sergeants disliked recruits in general, those like me in particular. Some recruits were identified as McNamara's War Morons. By 1968, America had run out of qualified draftees. The army lowered its qualification standards with the implementation of Secretary of Defense Robert McNamara's Project 100,000. Many of the draftees admitted under the new standards had been given a get-out-of-jail card in exchange for a tour in the army. Of course, some of those accepted prior to Project 100,000—Leadhead and Too Tall among them—were less than ideal versions of the exulted American fighting man.

With this in mind, Too Tall and I had pulled guard-duty, a bad assignment in the dead of a subzero Mannheim night. We were dug into the snow-thickened landscape, guarding the fort's outer perimeter. Accordingly, our superiors knew the importance of not arming Bible-eating Too-Tall, or for that matter, pot-head Pvt. Levine, with live ammo.

Too Tall's scream from his nearby smoke-filled fox-hole woke me. "Hey Levine, we've got guns but ain't got no bullets."

"Seems like a flawed concept, homeboy," I said. "Start rolling snowballs."

"O.K. Got any gloves over there?" he replied, then added, "Hey Levine, did you hear something out there?"

"I think I did," I said. "There's a bunch of them."

"Here they come, we've got to clear out— run Levine!"

I said nothing. There had been no approaching enemy voices or dinging of bullets, yet off he went, a rifle-toting Abominal Snowman, disappearing into the dark, not to be seen again for two days.

It was a defining moment.

Still, what the "Morons" lacked in formal education and moral rectitude, they made up for in taking to basic training where they learned such life skills—in combat they truly were life skills— as marksmanship, bayoneting and grenade tossing. In Advanced Infantry Training, they were schooled in such niceties as When and Where a Soldier Should Remove His Hat and How to Recognize a Prostitute. Only the latter proved beneficial in Mannheim.

I ate little, surviving mostly on junk food purchased from the PX, avoiding the mess hall, which frightened me more than even the unnerving thought of enemy fire. One featured item in the mess hall buffet was a quantity of chipped beef covered in warm milk served over warm bread, better known as Shit On A Shingle—and every bit as delicious. It looked, and smelled, like it had been previously consumed. Most privates drew occasional kitchen patrol duty, which also served as a loathed punishment. As a result, resentful food preparers in the predawn hours did uncivil things to the food their fellow soldiers soon would consume. C-rations doled out during field exercises were even worse. One member of my platoon contemplated the flavor of those tins of precooked meat much as a sommelier might a bottle of exquisite French wine and concluded it included hints of candied liver, powdered eggs, iodine, chewing gum, and stale cigarettes. I traded my rations for cigarettes, sold the smokes, and used the profits to fund my junk food habit.

Job mastery merited promotion, with about a one chance in six of transfer to Southeast Asia. Proficiency became Vietnam roulette. Superior performance was a spin of the chamber. Getting fired, as opposed to getting fired at, was pretty much impossible, but I made it my military goal. I engaged in a game of"Icant-doitisms"— a practice of intentional failure. I became competent at nothing, and my demonstrable incompetence perhaps ultimately saved my skin. I told no one, not even David, my strategy. Job mastery required a full two months at a minimum; I never held the same job more than six weeks. I bungled, in order, seven efforts to teach me a usable skill: reconnaissance scout, tank driver, machine gunner—how hard could that be?—mechanic, map reader, jeep driver and KP. It was risk and reward. I risked all possibility of promotion. I was rewarded with no ticket to Vietnam.

My life became survival of the unfittest. I became something of a pariah among the other men, the quintessential fuckup. All I wanted was to like what I had to do to achieve the secret to happiness and virtue. That wasn't going to happen in the Army. And a little love now and then was also on the list of my desires. There wasn't much hope of finding that, either.

Yet, I won't say Mannheim was hell, it was more like purgatory only because I knew someday I would get out.

The war effort in Vietnam spiked that year, while public support plummeted at home. In one particularly bloody week, more than three thousand American soldiers were killed or wounded. I felt no guilt that I was stationed in Europe and not in Southeast Asia. Still, the unpleasant thought of being sent to the latter always shadowed my mind.

I had assumed given my good fortune and better arm that my Army rank and title would be Pvt. Chuck Levine, Baseball Player. While no such position existed, I did make the Mannheim team and was on the field all of four innings during the entire ninety-day season. Athletic talent was irrelevant. Rank dictated who played. Sergeants and corporals took the field and privates rode the bench. We lost most of our games. The Cobras, as we were known although the venomous snakes weren't native to Germany—Southeast Asia, yes—played the game at about a high school caliber. I could have helped; baseball was something in which I had no problem displaying competence. I had after all traveled with a college all-star team and competed with and against future major leaguers. At season's end, I was assigned to the motor pool. I was okay with that; better that Philly Chuck Levine was fighting frozen bolts in Mannheim than gooks in the jungles of Vietnam.

EXCHANGE OF THOUGHTS

D avid, needless to say, adjusted to army life better than I did. Where I was negative and reactionary, he was negative and pragmatic. I expressed my anger. He internalized his. David espoused a levelheaded philosophy of use or be used. I listened and calmed down.

The more I learned about David, the more I understood how different our backgrounds truly were. His ideas were richly textured and not entirely because of his academic immersion. My ideas came from the roughage of a more commonplace existence. Yet, we shared intersections. He had deserted a woman named Marilyn. I had abandoned Sharon. And we drank, smoked, laughed, and shared thoughts we both for the most part had held inside. Neither of us truly knew much about women, but we were adept at discussing and trying to fathom them. Our friendship was an indispensable source of relief. He became my antidote to the tedium and absurdity of army life, and I his.

David switched weapons, putting down his gun and raising his pen. He didn't file his Conscience Objector Application until after being drafted and deployed. That order wasn't unheard of, but the process was unexampled. COs normally filed their applications before entering the military. Successful applicants were offered alternative civilian service. Corporal Craver had been in the army nearly ten months at the time that he submitted his application.

During the year-long application process, David was assigned a clerical position in which he typed up redeployment orders, which would send soldiers to their next assignment, which often involved a tour in Vietnam. He realized that doing so made him a cog, albeit minor, in the war machine. He conceded that by accepting this role in the military he was acting in a way that was, in his words, "fundamentally cowardly."

David had discovered that a soldier could petition for CO status as long as he had come to the realization that he conscientiously objected only after being drafted. He studied military law and decisions rendered. His objection, unlike most, was not based on his religion. His premise was that he simply, morally, and philosophically was incapable of killing other human beings. He wasn't even much for criticizing them

The CO approval process was based on three questions, and an applicant's fate was determined by how consistently he answered various subsets of each. The overarching questions were: What do you believe (about participation in war)? How did your beliefs develop (what events, factors influenced you to believe this)? And, lastly, How does your life reflect those beliefs (or how do your beliefs influence decisions or choices you make daily)? Skeptical as I was—and am—I more than suspected that an interviewer's mood and the interviewee's rank influenced the former's decisions. I based this on the futility of Miriam's diagnosis of me and the Lt. Cole fiasco. To my way of thinking, there was a risk that not all applicants would be treated alike even if their arguments were similar. David had to convince an officer that there was no rational basis for killing—that all lives had equal value—and to hope in the end that he would not hear, "You're the third man who has informed me of that today, Craver." David submitted his application and waited for an answer. Several months passed. David's paperwork was in the hands of military brass for review. We went about life with little talk of his application. I had concluded that he wished to escape the frustrating unknown, so I didn't pry. He awaited his fate while I continued to pursue my strategy of quantifiable incompetence.

The war worsened as 1968 gave way to 1969. During the latter, the same year that two Americans would land on the moon, another five hundred and fifty thousand American husbands, fathers, children, and lovers would be receiving their mail in Vietnam. Many would not live long enough to open it. The conflict by then had torn America apart. Anti-war protestors had moved beyond campuses onto city streets and the overflow was experienced in Germany. Discipline inside Coleman Barracks deteriorated. New arrivals made no attempt to hide their drug use, nor did the rest of us. We all wanted out of Germany. One of us one morning got his wish.

It was not long after Neil Armstrong took "One small step for man, one giant leap for mankind," that David got the news. He woke me early one August morning by shaking my bunk. "I'm out! I'm out!" he shouted. "I'm out!" I turned to face him, his meaning not immediately registering. Then I realized what he was saying, David was out of the Army. I bounced off the cot and we did a celebratory jig. Despite my doubts about the process, I had believed from the beginning that his communication skills would earn him his escape, and I had been proven right. He had written his way out of the Army during time of war, a rare accomplishment. His freedom awaited him.

His intelligence and love of language would serve him well in civilian life, where he belonged all along. I was happy for him and grateful for the time we had had together, during which I had learned a good deal. I wondered if he had similarly benefitted in some fashion. I wanted to offer something more than congratulations, but was momentarily deprived of words. David came to the rescue. "Come stay with my family when you get out," he invited. "I'll meet you at Fort Dix. Think it over."

It took me a matter of seconds to accomplish that. I had but four months remaining until my discharge. I was too "short" for a Vietnam tour, and now that I had an East Coast connection, I wasn't returning to California. Other than that, my future was unmapped, all roads fogged in.

David suggested I visit his cousin Tom in England before returning to the states. David said he would speak with him and would keep me posted.

Mail call took on a new relevance. In mid-November, a letter arrived from David informing me that Tom and his family were looking forward to hosting me in Southampton. I was delighted. Of course, with a bloody and senseless war going on, other news arrived that was decidedly less pleasant. Freeman received a letter from Corporal Medina a week before I left. Medina had lost a leg in

Vietnam. So much for his discounted motorcycle. I idly wondered if his deposit was refundable. I felt for him, particularly now that I was days away from escaping alive and intact.

Fourteen days of army life remained; on December 12, 1969, I would again be a free man. I had not been granted leave in my seventeen months in Germany. Two requests had been turned down due to "behavior unbecoming an enlisted soldier." I had no argument for that, yet on November 30, I was granted a ten-day pass. Finally, I left post, on my feet not my belly, and walked to the southbound side of A4. The road sign read Paris 519 km. I stuck my right thumb skyward. I was merely hitching a ride, but it felt appropriate to signal a thumbs up.

I had dodged Vietnam and I had survived the workaday melancholy of Mannheim. In a few weeks I was going to New York, to a place I'd never been. I assured myself that whatever lay ahead was manageable. It was time for me to get on with life.

Call it karma, serendipity, godsend, or luck; the following day into the night was the most remarkable in my life to that point. I was in Paris, eating cheeses fit for a king, drinking wine that was nothing less than elixir, and met a woman named Sarah. Mannheim? Never heard of it, and New York could wait. Then she went her way, and dazed I floated by ferry from Calais to Dover. Tom met me at the terminal. He showed off his Mini-Cooper's performance during the brisk drive to Southampton.

Tom's family and I ate crumpets with tea in the mornings. Bangers wrapped in The London Times made for a fine lunch. We drank warm beer and threw darts in pubs at night. I slept in a real bed. First Sarah and then this. I realized I had forgotten pleasure and drank of it in gulps. Neither Tom nor his wife blew a six a.m. whistle. We discussed everything from Winston Churchill's life to American football. I audited one of Tom's lectures at Southampton University. One afternoon I saw "Midnight Cowboy," which had been censored from Coleman's movie list. The film further fueled me for life in New York. I thanked my hosts for their hospitality beyond anything I could I have presumed and then stopped off briefly in London before returning to Mannheim. I was fully revived.

Two days later, I boarded a flight to Fort Dix, New Jersey. Private E-2 Charles Levine had survived the awful war in Germany. I had had one at bat in two years. I hadn't fielded a single ground ball. I hadn't ducked a single knock-down pitch, nor had I brushed a man off the plate. But, most importantly, I had neither ducked nor thrown a hand grenade in combat. The Vietnam War would drag on, its casualties mounting for several more years, but my war was over.

THE PERFECT COCKTAIL

D avid collected me from the discharge station at Fort Dix. I
changed into my much-abused long-sleeved red shirt, tan
khakis, and black loafers. I left my boots and uniform behind
in the men's room. It was late Sunday night when bars in New
Jersey were ostensibly closed. After hugs and shouts and delir-
ious laughter, David suggested we have a drink. A heavy snow
was falling sideways as we stepped outside. Floodlights lit up the
ice-covered parking lot. We skated to David's car, a yellow VW
bug, and I squeezed into the passenger seat. One headlamp worked,
the other flickered when we hit a bump in the road. Squeaky windshield wipers drowned out the radio and the bent radio antenna
flopped in the wind. It was the greatest car in the world, it was
carrying me into the town of my liberation. David took the interstate and after forty-five minutes turned off it and we drove another
mile on a gravel road. The car bottomed out with a bang and jarred
me into reality as we passed under a trestle. Suddenly, I wasn't
thinking of Mannheim any more but of mysterious excitement that
lay ahead. This was a juncture in my life. I felt energized, excited
by whatever was next although I had no idea what it was. David
pulled the Beetle to the curb in front of The Prince of Whales in
Perth Amboy. I unfolded my body and got out.

The Prince was a crusty bar that still catered to seamen and
other hard-boiled sorts. A plastic sign over the entrance boasted that
it had been where it stood, "Since 1844." It was almost exactly the
same size, the same dimensions, as the barracks I had put behind
me. Loud, unruly men packed the room. Returning fishermen and
local rowdies were here to drink, make noise and, inevitably fight.
A respectable woman hadn't set foot in this dive in years. The only

difference between it and Coleman, it seemed to me, was that I could leave whenever the hell I wished.

Nothing was fancy, except a once handsome, now grime-stained mahogany bar that paralleled a mirrored wall, whales carved into its surface. Photographs featured men and the fish they had hauled up from the depths. The floor was covered in sawdust. It felt like America.

We sat at the bar. The keep was short and grossly obese. His equally bulbous nose canted to the left. A black patch hid his left eye. His right was blue and scar-lidded. His white apron identified him as Louie. I asked him why his regulars called him Jack.

"Louie's got da night off. What can I get ya?"

David ordered for us both, the house special, and Jack mixed two New Jersey Squirrels, one part Almond Liqueur, one of Applejack and a dash of lemon juice. The place was perfect for the moment. So, too, was the cocktail.

NEW YORK CITY

I left my humble, cosseted Sacramento background with limited social exposure only to be similarly limited by eighteen sheltered months of military life. My mother had supported me through adolescence, and the army had taken care of my basic needs afterward. Now I was on my own. A return to Sacramento was out of the question. At twenty-five, I wanted to establish myself as myself and develop materially and intellectually. New York had seemed the place from watching The Naked City. The great city intimidated me—I felt ill-equipped for whatever challenges lay ahead—yet I was drawn to its vast unknown. I decided to give New York a go.

My life was going to change. I felt it.

On a freezing January morning in 1969, I arrived in The Naked City. This was my long-anticipated episode. It featured Broadway plays, Yankees games, fine dining, beautiful women, Carnegie Hall, The Metropolitan Museum, Little Italy, The West Village, and more beautiful women, and I was loaded; I had fully one hundred and eighty-seven dollars in my wallet.

I had stayed briefly with the Cravers in New Jersey. The family home was as David had described it, an old, rambling, country farmhouse alongside a two-story barn perched on a hill. The house had a rustic yet stately feel. It held pleasing quirks found only in old, comfortable houses. The air around it carried wisps of burned wood and cooking odors and hints of mildew and an old dog. The wooden floor squeaked in a welcoming way. Its many windows this time of year looked out over snow-covered ground studded with dormant red oak trees. I loved the warmth and illumination of the fireplace defying the cold outside. Still, after two weeks, it was time for citizen Levine to see if and how I might fit into New York City.

David and I drove the five miles from Chapel Hill to Red Bank. He parked his bug, and we boarded an early bus to New York. I took a right-hand window seat on the northbound coach. Outside, it was bitterly cold. Plows had packed snow deep along the Garden State Parkway, the remains of that month's infamous nor'easter, which had buried long and wide swaths of New England beneath forty inches of heavy snow. The bus headed out shortly after dawn, and the sky slowly lightened beneath patches of dark and light clouds. A copy of that day's New York Times lay folded in my lap. I was excited and happy to be so. I worked to suppress a grin.

The coachman drove with his left hand at 12 o'clock on the orange, horizontal steering wheel. He held a blue Mets coffee mug in his right. He stopped several times along the fifty-mile route into the great city. At each stop, he shifted the mug to his left hand and with his right pushed the levered mechanism that opened and with a reverse pull closed the passenger door to accommodate the seemingly never-ending stream of dark-suited businessmen who came out of the cold into the bus's welcoming warmth. Each looked the same and carried attaches that looked all alike. I imagined a production line producing these serious, confident, interchangeable men and the conveyor belts that bore them to their individual bus stops like clockwork, just in time to board. Only rarely did one mutter a good morning to the driver, who pulled then on the door lever, its hydraulic action expelling an audible sigh over the idling engine. He shifted his transport into gear, and with a slight lurch forward and a bump as he pressed on the accelerator, we were off again to our shared destination.

The passengers were white, their shoes polished beyond even military requirement. Only the hues and designs of their ties suggested individuality. Some read newspapers, others began the workday, presumably jotting notes for the hours ahead. Each was to his own. They seemed to lift their heads from their work only to look up from their ubiquitous yellow pads, staring blankly ahead, lips pursed, in search of some thought or answer or another. The bus was as quiet as a church before the liturgy begins. The detachment our fellow riders shared was my first exposure to non-military management, a prelude to my immersion in private competition. It left me uncomfortable. I had no desire to be any of them yet envied their seeming success.

Twenty or so miles on, the New Jersey countryside changed its nature and the clouds further gave way as though taking some cue. I took a long pull on my Tareyton and wondered if one of these suited men—surely among the suits were an adman or two—had written the grammatically jarring ad that nevertheless sold millions on the brand: "Us Tareyton smokers would rather fight than switch!" The trademarked line accompanied doctored photos of Tareyton smokers, each with a black eye. That's how serious they— we—were about not giving up our cork-filtered brand. I turned my eyes back outside to the cityscape appearing on the eastern horizon.

We were closing in on a city—I guessed it had to be Weehawken because I knew it lay on this side of the tunnel that would carry us beneath the Hudson into New York City—and a certain truth became evident. New York, something concrete but not, given that I had envisioned and imagined it for so long that it had come to seem no more real than Oz, was in fact a real place, a frightening, exhilarating Mecca. What had appeared as scale models in the distant grew into towers as we closed in on it. And well even before we hit the tunnel, there it was in all its grandeur, and now for me it was only exhilarating. Skyscrapers, those temples of the city's economic might, stretched skyward. Mighty bridges along the length of the river struck me as a chain of anchors holding the island and its massive architecture in place. I'm convinced today as I was that morning that no one, be it by bus or sea or air, ever forgets their first glimpse of magnificent Manhattan.

The bus then plunged into darkness as it slipped into the Lincoln Tunnel. We emerged on the east side of the river and arrived at the Port Authority Bus Terminal on Eighth Avenue between Fortieth and Forty-second streets. It is the largest-such terminal in the United States, the busiest in the world. David and I were two of the sixty-nine million passengers who passed through it that year alone.

That morning of January 2, 1969, was clear and sunny and crisp. We stepped out onto Eighth Avenue. For a moment, I stood on the sidewalk— staring dazedly at its bright reflection. The thrill and pace of human activity all but took my breath away. I stopped and watched it pass, determined, purposeful, and quick. Fellow travelers brushed against me. Hatted heads, bouncing in rhythm with clicking heels, hustled past as if all were late to get to wherever they were going. There were, I assumed, among them the bankers and lawyers and engineers and merchants and admen all in a rush to squeeze in the work of a new day to kick start the new year.

And, too, and oddly reassuring, was a bearded street person in the company of his scraggly dog; it was an assurance to me that even if you failed you could succeed in surviving in this wild metropolis. The man held a sign that read "Food not Bombs" and cried out, "I have nightmares about the babies, and don't want to go to prison!" He and the better groomed managed to ignore one another. I was, just that quickly, in love with this place, where the locally born and the nation's drawn diaspora shared one tiny spot in the great, grand world, all the while existing universes apart from one another.

David nudged me and began to walk and I took a long step and caught up. We maneuvered through the masses wordlessly, except for those bouncing around my mind. Was I, an imposter, incapable of competing here? And how would I compete if I could? I wasn't going to be playing for the Yankees, not even for the less storied Mets. This was the World Series of life.

I had no job, no connections, no education to speak of and but a single friend. Yet, a vital zing, the energy of the city, was surfacing, an unrealized energy I waited to join. I was in New York City, open to The Naked City's possibilities, game to write my story among the other millions here. And if I failed, no one anywhere else would need know, nor would they ask. I wouldn't be beseeched with questions about jobs I hadn't landed, or about the career I hadn't pursued, or about the story I had failed to tell.

I was still caught up, but soon enough I began to gather my bearings. Those first few minutes had overwhelmed me. Only after a while did I realize that because The Naked City had been filmed in black and white I had perceived New York as such. The real story I saw was in color. And the real city moved more quickly in person then it had on screen.

I took inventory. I had now a little less than a hundred and fifty dollars, a single change of clothes, no experience to speak of and even less confidence to draw on. Yet, the possibilities advertised themselves as unlimited. Had I headed home to Sacramento, what would I have done? Resumed working at Mack's? No, whatever this city held was where I would begin anew. There, I would most likely have been a minor cog in a wheel, expendable, unfulfilled. Here, the cogs might grind me to nothing, but it was a grander mechanism, a superior machination, and I was now, naively, foolishly, unconditionally committed to giving this a go. I quickly committed to whatever sacrifices were necessary. Sure, I wanted to go out, hit the spots, drink, smoke, get laid, and otherwise be licentious, but that would have to wait. I had gleaned that New York was a place Darwin might have studied in devising his theory of survival of the fittest.

New York was a place where the established were cautious to the extreme, and those new to it were willing to risk their all to join the established. New York was a city peopled by aristocrats and hobos, by clowns and monsters, and all sorts imaginable and beyond imagination in between. Many excelled at what they did, others at what they didn't do. Awareness and energy advanced dreams. An abundance of money helped. Opportunity electrified the air, as lightning does before thunder fills the vacuum the bolts create.

Having felt stilted in my hometown and stifled in Mannheim, I felt aware and awakened in Manhattan. Like anyone still too callow not to be compromising in my ideas, I was excessive in my enthusiasms and extreme in my ambitions. I knew I would survive, but, like anyone, I wanted more than that. I had picked fruit with the braceros during long Sacramento Valley summers. I had no doubts about my work ethic, but I had doubts that I would find something in this vast, fantastic city that would fulfill me. I did know that something was here for me. What I didn't know was what and when I would find it. I felt through my reverie David's gaze.

"Well?" he asked.

"Yes," I said.

"Good. Let's get something to eat."

Manhattan became my home for the next three and a half years. Never did I become a commuter, nor did I ever sleep on the street. I did, however, live in a flophouse as I began this new journey. I got robbed, I drove a taxi, and I sold plastic, which required that I change my name. And, too, I got married, brushed against the underworld, and met Suzy the flying dog. Surviving forty-two months in New York, I discovered, will gird anyone for life.

I moved into an eight-story walkup—albeit on the second floor— on Twenty-sixth Street just off Lexington Avenue, which cost me all of twenty-six dollars a month. The room, five feet by eight feet, was tighter than a jail cell, but I could leave it as I desired. It seemed a fair enough compromise. A window opened into a light well, down which dropped wine bottles, condoms, hypodermic needles, and leftovers warmly received by the rats below. A bed, a night-stand, and a clothes hanger filled my room. A communal toilet with wooden shower stalls was down the hallway. Once, while out and about I met a lovely Pan Am stewardess at an Upper East Side bar and invited her home. There was no second date.

I made fleeting friends with some of my transient neighbors while sharing the stoop out front. Smelly Bob Spinelli was down on his luck. Bob was in his thirties and recently separated and was gainfully employed as a janitor—he preferred the title of san-itary engineer—at the Empire State Building. After paying his rent and diner tabs, the rest of his income went to his "lousy fucking wife and her kids." Bob was from Jersey and the year I made his acquaintance went home for Christmas with presents he had bought from a street vendor, neatly packaged "Cashmere sweaters," which when opened proved to have no backs.

Phil Shumanski was destined to die on the streets. He was the only paranoid schizophrenic I have ever known to my knowledge. I liked being around him but never got too close. His fingernails matched the color and scuff of his black shoes. He was intelli-gent, but vexed by voices only he heard. Phil was fifty years old and claimed to have the world's greatest collection of Russian lit-erature "outside the Kremlin." He was hiding his foreign library, he one day told me, from the Federal Bureau of Investigation— which he never referred to as the FBI—which he assured me was watching both of us as we sat on the steps. He advised me not to look up to where they were looking down. Phil credited his disinterest in women to Sigmund Freud. Freud, he said, explained that females' dangling earrings represented the testicles they had been born without—proof, he said, of their testicle envy. I was left to wonder on my own what they might be wearing to express penis envy. Phil one bitter January night fell asleep in the snow in front of our building and at the emergency room several of his frostbitten fingers were removed.

And, too, there were in our building a bearded man who dressed in a pink fairy's costume with flapping, silk wings and traversed the streets on roller skates, and Tina, who smoked cigars and adroitly spun plates on sticks, and my friend and favorite, sixty-year old "Officer" Cargo, who directed traffic with his whistle and spinning arms, always wearing what I took to be a 1920s-era police uniform and a Jets football helmet. To me, they were innocents and enhanced the city I had embraced. They brought theater out of the theater and onto the street.

One day, I watched Cargo make all manner of mayhem at the intersection of West Fifty-fourth Street and Sixth Avenue, where he conducted an otherwise unruly orchestra through a tremolo involving the full horn section. When the light turned green on Sixth Avenue, he shrilled two rapid tweets of his whistle, elevated his arms skyward and vigorously wheeled his arm in the only direction motorists could go on the one-way street. As the light again turned red, Cargo, in a blur and a bounce, leapt and motioned clear the way for the pedestrians who were already well into the intersection. Meanwhile, cross-town traffic on Fifty-fourth barreled past him on his right as he whirled them through.

I was, in a certain way, no different than Cargo, Phil and Smelly Spinelli, we were all finding our way to the best of our abilities in a city that both embraced and ignored us. We found among us a certain sense of community and genuine companionship; we were together and not alone. It helped perhaps that I had nothing worth stealing. I stayed on Twenty-sixth Street into the following year as the 1960s gave way to a new decade and a new promise of new opportunity. I kept my room tidy and clean and my window closed save for the rare evening when the breeze blew just right and bore nothing foul. I enjoyed my stay there. Yes, I was poor but I was free and on my own and whatever I made of the future wasn't yet the moment I was in. WOR's Jean Shepherd entertained my evenings in a way reminiscent of how KFBK's Tony Koester had back in Sacramento in what now seemed an era past.

Shepherd told humorous tales of childhood and of his own time in the army, of baseball and of the swells and dips that populated New York. With Shep in the background, I sat on my bed and filled out job applications beneath the dim luminosity of a fifty-watt bulb.

CAREER SEEDS

Less than a month into New York, I caught a break, landing a minor position on Park Avenue. The Sinclair Koppers Company hired me as a "liaison." I don't know what they saw in me, nor did I have a full grasp on just what a liaison actually did. I had shoulder-length hair and a bushy mustache. I looked more like Sonny Bono than I did the clean-cut junior executives surrounding me.

My daily trek from Twenty-sixth Street to the office on Sixty-third and Park Avenue was a highlight of my day, each street a separate stage, each act its own. There were dogs leashed to their doppelganger masters; a beggar embraced by a boa constrictor; a monk in his robes and Ferragamo shoes; prophets' dire warnings of hell's fire should the lesson of John 3:16 be ignored greeted me at the bottom of the Lexington, Madison and Park Avenue canyons. I walked through and past this carnival with a certain joy most mornings until I arrived at the building that housed Koppers'office. It didn't take long before that arrival filled me with dread, a pervasive sense of doom that grew as the elevator carried me to the twelfth floor.

My position as a liaison called for writing apology letters to disappointed customers of Koppers' pool paints. Most of their complaints were not, to be honest, the company's fault, but rather were due to contractors' misapplication of the products, perhaps not allowing the first coat to dry before applying the second, or failing to prime a pool's surface, or using the wrong applicator. It soon became apparent that competent contractors were in the minority. New complaints, many accompanied by threats of civil lawsuits, arrived daily. I did my best to console the authors and often thought I would be better employed writing to the contractors. That would be a terse epistle. It would read, in its entirety: "Read the label, dumbkoff."

I suggested to my boss—my bosses—that that would prove a better use of my time and of their investment in me, but that made clear wasn't going to happen and at any rate I soon realized I had no future with Koppers. Still, I stayed on while taking a second job as a sales clerk at Bloomingdale's. That allowed me to begin saving money and, more importantly, meeting women. I worked evenings in the Maud Shop, selling paisley shirts and ties. The multi-colored, feather-shaped patterns evoked psychedelia and appealed to acid-dripping '70s hipsters. Everything from wallpaper to VW buses was dressed in paisley as were those men who embraced the design. Most of the women shopping at the Maud Shop were young women shopping for their men.

One day, a woman named Paula Weinstein came in and bought a shirt and a few days later returned and sought me out and asking me again to help her sort out the offerings on the rack bought another paisley shirt, albeit larger. I gave her my employee discount, and she gave me the shirt—and her phone number. We began dating although we had nothing in common. I lived in a flophouse, smoked pot from time to time, and now wore a paisley shirt. Paula rented a brownstone, drank wine and wore solids. We knew from the start that we would become one another's discards. Until then though we were lovers absent love. We never disagreed, yet the thought of continuing our relationship afflicted us both. Nevertheless, we kept it up the better part of a year.

Paula and I had been dating, if that's the word, I can think of others, for a couple of months when I got the break that would become my career. Paula had introduced me to a friend of hers who owned a company named Almac Plastics, in Long Island City. Almac fabricated and distributed plastic sheets, rods, tubes and film. I applied for a job and was interviewed by the human resources manager, a slight man named Stan Willis, who had been born Stanley Hoffmeyer. Our conversation went well, and Stan gave me a nod and introduced me to Mike Brown, the plant manager, whose real name was Michael Weinberg. Brown clapped me on the back and told me I was "good material," and introduced me to the man who ran the office and was ultimately responsible for the final vetting of potential new hires, a fellow named Jerry Conner, whose parents still remembered him as Harold Schiffman. A few days later, I was invited to meet with Almac's vice president, Mr. G., who was known at his synagogue as Gerry Goldman.

Mr. Conner told me he had heard nothing but good things about me and wanted nothing more than to accept me into the fold if I wouldn't mind carrying with me a business card that identified me as someone else. I agreed, reversed my initials, and Larry Chambers was born. No one explained why the name change. I thought it was a sexy idea. I was a new person in town. The newest of eight million. Why not be someone else? If Larry Chambers failed I could start over as Charles Levine, or maybe Chuck. The year before I was drafted into the army, "The Graduate" was released and the character played by Dustin Hoffman had been advised that the future lay in "just one word ... plastics," and I had never forgotten that advice. Better Larry Chambers sell plastic, I figured, than Charles Levine continue to soothe pissed-off pool-paint purchasers. Beside, Hoffman's character had gotten laid by Anne Bancroft.

Larry Chambers worked Manhattan the next three years, passing out hundreds of personalized business cards, reserving tables under his assigned name—"Hello, Mr. Chambers, always a pleasure to see you; I think you'll like tonight's special"—and selling a hell of a lot of plastic. I, we, were now gentiles, passing as such, and though I had never been observant, I squirmed in my new identity but appreciated that Larry Chambers was making a respectable living. I knew only a few fellow New Yorkers who knew me as Charles Levine, among them David Craver, whom I now saw only occasionally. I was busy selling plastic, and he was busy working as a reporter for the Petroleum Intelligence Weekly, writing about the crude product that when refined produced among other byproducts, ethylene, the feedstock for everything I sold.

At last I was making decent money but no great fortune, and so I took on a second job, a night job, seeing and working the city from behind the wheel of a cab. After all, you can't sell plastic after the buyers take the train home.

DRIVER, HEY DRIVER!

In 1970, the year I began augmenting my income as a hack, seven New York cab drivers were killed and another three thousand, the lucky ones, were merely robbed. I was one of five thousand wheelmen for hire at night, all of us driving the streets in our distinctive yellow cabs, the light above the roof beckoning to all who needed a lift.

It took me a while to learn Manhattan's streets and varied alleys. I carried on my lap a city map and held a flashlight close to hand. I enjoyed the hell out of the work. Taxi drivers get asked questions of all sorts, their passengers take them to be savants, knowledgeable on all fronts. Tourists relied on their expertise, asking, say, "Is the food better at the Russian Tea Room or at Delmonico's." I told the Soviets that the Tea Room was preferable, and the Italians that Delmonico's was my preference. Single men and, to a lesser extent, women wanted to know where the action was. Businessmen and -women just wanted me to keep my mouth shut. Tips sometimes hinged on a firm answer to an impossible question. From time to time I was asked, "Which airplanes are safest, the ones at JFK, or those flying out of La Guardia?" And—typically this came from couples who looked like they were from Iowa, or maybe Nebraska—someone might ask, "Where can I see the Mafia guys?" I learned quickly that "I don't know" was the wrong answer. As for JFK as opposed to La Guardia, it depended on which was further away. I took those interested in spotting a goodfella to Little Italy and always advised them to keep their heads down and their eyes open.

Artists, students, businessmen and tourists alike, I soon learned, smoked pot. Sharing mine was part of the service, sometimes resulting in extraordinary tips. With my long hair and mustache, I looked like a doper. I often enough asked clients, "Do you have a preferred route?" or, "You want a hit?" More than one adventurous tourist took his first toke in my cab. Two guys from somewhere in Indiana got ripped in my cab on the way to the airport. The Maui Waui had hit them hard by the time we arrived at La Guardia. They argued over who was richer and neither able to cede the point, both insisted on paying the fare. Who was I to object? I collected fares from both. I truly loved the job.

Cab drivers, like deer during hunting season, depend on keen senses. He first must assess the potential fare, ideally spotting hunters before allowing them in and weighing their stated destinations—"Take me anywhere into the park" was never good.

Yet, regardless of one's experience and capacity to learn, there were predators that prey never saw coming. One night in my first month behind the wheel, both front windows down on a hot, late night, I pulled over on the Upper East Side at the raise of a handsome, well-dressed man's hand, his voice addressing me as my cab slowed: "Driver, hey driver!" He was in his mid twenties and had on a sharp, gray, double-breasted suit. He gave me an address uptown. We had gone no more than a block before he told me to cut through the park via Seventy-second Street to Columbus Avenue on the west side. I told him that was the wrong direction to his destination. He repeated the request, now a demand, and in the rear view I saw his hand reach into his left-hand inner jacket pocket. I floored it and spun a U-turn and headed south onto northbound Third Avenue. Never mind that the speed limit was twenty-five. I was moving well past forty when he shouted, "Jesus christ! Let me out, you crazy sonofabitch!" I slammed on the brakes and my passenger banged his head on the plastic divider between us. I jumped out, and he limped out, and I got back in as he rubbed his forehead, and to this day he owes me two dollars and ninety five cents. And, yes, perhaps he was up to nothing. Who knows? Who cares?

My share of every fare and every tip I hustled went into a savings account I had set up for that purpose. I lived off my day job. The work took me into nooks and crannies of the city that held a fascination. I enjoyed driving up and down Manhattan and, too, across the bridges into the other boroughs. I felt an affection for the people, an appreciation for the architecture, a curiosity of all the city suggested. My emerging awareness that anything might happen at any time was exhilarating. This was New York. It was my home.

My Calling

A lmac Plastics put me through a vigorous, albeit less than rigorous, training program. I enhanced it with my own study
of the company's product literature. Initially the sales manager,
Lee Stafford, who was really Reginald Cohen, joined me on sales
calls, which at first were confined to Brooklyn. I was good at it, and
within two months I was turned loose in Manhattan.

It was a glorious job. I inherited some key accounts and devel-
oped others. In 1972 I was told to visit Continental Oil's Connecticut
headquarters. Selling Continental Oil was my biggest coup. I went
armed with specs for a custom, very expensive, plastic floor mat
for the CEO's expansive office. After showing him the sketches, I
asked the chief executive, with a joking friendliness, if anyone else
occupying one of the corner offices deserved a similar floor mat;
the commission, I told him, might just cover my train fare back to
Manhattan. He laughed and joked that I should come back in a year
and ask him again. I marked my calendar and visited him to the
day. To my pleasure, and, too, to my astonishment, he remembered
me and saw me despite that I hadn't made an appointment. Oddly
enough, Continental Oil just so happened to be refurbishing a 200-
office commercial building. I walked out of my meeting with the
largest chair mat order in Almac's history.

The Museum of Modern Art, The Metropolitan and other
museums bought plastic from me. I called on the New York Stock
Exchange, the then new World Trade Center, on Carnegie Hall and
Broadway theaters, movie companies, major hotels, department
stores, and city agencies. I convinced many of them that Almac
and I had just what they needed. I had found my calling in life. I
had always doubted myself and now was coming to understand
that others didn't. I had landed in this strange, new place full of

uncertainty. Sale by sale, that gave way to newfound confidence. I was making a name for myself in the company's—and the country's—toughest market. I began to think about daring to go out on my own.

By then, I had moved from my flophouse and my unusual friends to an apartment on Eighty-sixth Street between West End Avenue and Riverside Drive. I had met a woman named Susan, a gentle and pleasant woman from Long Island. We were less compatible than Paula and I had been but she was kind and forgave my rough edges and over time we decided to marry. Five years and one blessed child later, we divorced.

In the early 1970s, the plastics industry was booming, and I had absorbed the advice The Graduate's Benjamin Braddock had been offered—"Just one word. Are you listening?" "Yes, I am." "Plastics"—and I now gave considerable thought to going out on my own, but did nothing rash. For the next three years, I continued to sell for Almac while learning everything I could. I knew New York was out of the question; Almac had that market. I thought about where I might succeed on my own. I considered Atlanta and Seattle and Los Angeles before settling on San Francisco. I researched my potential customer base and suppliers. Armed with nothing more than optimism and my not altogether insignificant savings, Susan and I packed our belongings and our cat, Tiffany, into a U-Haul truck. The California plastics rush was on.

A RETURN HOME

M ark Twain is credited—though not alone—with noting that the American nature is optimistic, that the moment may be hard, but the future surely will be better. I believed he was right. I had gone to New York in search of a career I knew nothing of, not its parameters nor its nature, and I had found it. Now, I sought to build on what had come my way.

The three of us found a place—at 2222 22nd Avenue—its symmetry somehow suggesting something fortuitous. This was in 1974. The day we took the apartment in the Sunset District, between Rivera and Santiago streets, was warm and the sky blue and the temperature in the sixties. It felt like something I have never believed in: It felt like heaven. We had paid two hundred and fifty dollars in New York for a six-hundred-square-foot studio in Lincoln Center. We paid the same in San Francisco for three times the space and a garage and a floral backyard. The City's resonant foghorns replaced Manhattan's wailing sirens. Valleys lay at the foot of The City's seven hills rather than the canyons that lay between New York's skyscrapers. Everyone in The City, even the losers, was winning or emerging. The Golden State Warriors that year won the NBA Championship. A kid born in San Francisco named O.J. Simpson led the Buffalo Bills to the NFL playoffs, the only year he ever played beyond the regular season; Joe Montana, who would become a San Francisco legend, matriculated to Notre Dame; and the San Francisco Giants outfielder Bobby Bonds's son Barry, who would become the greatest home-run hitter of all time while wearing a Giants uniform, turned ten. And, on June 10, Pacific Coast Plastics came into being, starting out in a garage at 7 Natoma Street. The sun that day broke through the fog for the last time until September. The clouds that had begun to obscure our marriage never did lift.

Susan and I worked long hours—hers even longer, given that she took charge over the rearing of our son, Scott, who was born the year after our company had been—me spending time with vendors, making sales calls, cutting and delivering product, collecting receivables, while she saw to the books. Susan was a wonderful and meticulous bookkeeper—this in the days before personal computers eased the burden. She had learned double-entry bookkeeping working for Seventeen magazine and incorporated those skills into our system. We invested all but our meager living expenses back into the company.

Perhaps it was the struggle to raise a son and build a company or that we were irreconcilable or that divorce is heritable—I've never determined which—but Susan and I parted four years later. I paid her for her share of the company, of which I then became the sole proprietor. We shared custody of Scott.

What had been a mom and pop company was now a pop-alone business. The company grew despite my mistakes, the biggest of which was that I defied an accepted maxim: Don't mix business with pleasure. My business crossed—became—my social life. I rented a penthouse on Nob Hill, drove a Ferrari, and dated some of my female clients. I knew I was in trouble. I recognized that my new friends liked me for what I offered them, not for whom I was. My lifelong battle with insecurity became a war in my mind. I began to think back to my time in Mannheim and my friendship with David Craver, a bond I had never doubted, one built on mutual appreciation of our shared entrapment.

A decade had passed since our Mannheim days and I questioned still his reasons for befriending me. I was succeeding in business but remained uncertain of myself, and of my relationship with those around me other than my son, who I knew loved me without reservation as only small children do.

An Altering Evening

O ne autumn night in 1981, I went out to dinner with a childhood buddy named Michael. We had gone our separate ways after high school. He had been more intellectual and ambitious than I could have imagined and had become a psychologist. We had reconnected after my return to California and got together a couple times a year to reminisce and to catch up. We shared an interest in sports and often also talked about our careers and families, his whole, mine divided. We agreed that night to meet for dinner at the Northern-Italian-style restaurant Prego.

I had parked on a hill rising on Buchanan Street, backing in and turning my wheels to insure the tires caught the curb. I stepped out onto the lamp-lit street and into the quiet, cool evening. Our reservation was for eight p.m. I was thirty minutes early. Prego was three blocks away. Fog overhead pushed past the Cow Hollow rooftops. I walked down steep Buchanan while trying to envision Prego's menu; failing, I turned to recalling its cocktail list, and proved more adept. Roasting garlic lured me to Prego's entrance, where I saw Michael, early too, reviewing the street-posted menu beside the door.

We shook hands and I clapped his shoulder. We went inside. The hostess seated us to one side of a fireplace. Our table faced the room and my back was to the wall. Michael sat to my left facing the bar. We ordered martinis. He updated me on his accomplished wife and his disappointment that Forty-Niner Cedrick Hardman had crossed the bay and was now an Oakland Raider. Michael had named his dog Cedrick. The waiter stood a moment before interrupting and took our orders. We both started with a Caesar salad. I ordered sautéed sand dabs and Michael went for the risotto with clams. We ignored tradition and ordered a cabernet. Our waiter raised an eyebrow before assuring us we had made a most excellent choice. Michael was the sort of old friend you don't see for months and yet it seems just yesterday since last yakking. We toasted often and laughed all the more. All the while I kept one eye on two attractive women, one auburn, the other's hair black, seated nearby, their table canted in such a way that both half faced us. One looked back. She had pale, clear skin and shoulder-length, black hair and a tiny, upturned nose. We shared a brief smile and nothing more.

Michael and I left the restaurant at ten, and I sensed I had left something behind.

"You forget something?"

"Yeah. I'll be right back."

He sensed what I was thinking and followed me back in. We approached the two women, and I introduced us. Their names were Maura and Mary. They were cousins and best friends and roommates. I glanced at Maura's naked ring finger even as she invited us to sit. I was more than a bit drunk and declined her offer, afraid I'd make an ass of myself and that would be that. I managed to say, stupidly, "Maybe we'll see you here again sometime."

She again invited us to sit, and Michael thanked her and pulled back a chair and sat. I had no choice but to do the same. We talked briefly about what we did for work and how long each and all had lived in The Bay Area and where in the Bay Area we lived. By then I had moved to Marin County, north of The City across the Golden Gate Bridge, on which only one man had died during its decade-long construction until in the final year ten men plunged to their deaths all at once. I ordered a bottle of wine, still as nervous as a teenager, and halfway through a glass began to relax. The four of us laughed and agreed we lived in the most wonderful city and all along I looked for a graceful way to make my exit. I looked at my watch and hoped I appeared startled at where the time had gone and stood and expressed my pleasure at meeting both. Maura forthrightly asked for a card and Michael threw down his Visa onto the table. We all laughed and I relaxed and sat again. I was taken with Maura's intelligence and forward nature and hoped no one else noticed that she was the only one I saw.

TRANSFORMATION

The drive home took thirty-five minutes. Crossing the Golden Gate, I reassessed my new life. I had given up my hedonistic impulses and had quit snorting cocaine—I did still smoke a bit of pot—and had moved to Mill Valley, fragrant with its old-growth pines and alive with its history and, too, its newfound wealth, and had, title and all, given the Ferrari to a loyal and valued employee named Lee, who had followed me from New York. The company was doing well and I felt serene in Mill Valley's embrace, and was missing only someone with whom to share my rising success and increasingly comfortable life. I fell asleep that night thinking of Maura.

She remained on my mind over the weekend and was on my mind when I headed to work Monday morning. I regretted not having asked her for her card. Monday became Tuesday and Tuesday Wednesday and though the phone rang fifty times a day, it was never Maura on the other end. I gathered that she wasn't going to call and that I would always cradle a memory of someone I had fallen for and had failed to woo and I found myself shaking my head in disdain. On that week's Thursday, the usual stack of banded mail arrived in the office, vendors' catalogs and more importantly the sustenance of Pacific Coast Plastics, receipts and bills, which I thumbed through and separated into two piles, and junk mail, which I deposited in the trash can beneath my desk—and an envelope that because it was handwritten caught my eye. Inside was a note card on embossed stock that read:

"Dear Charles, It was nice meeting you. I would enjoy getting to see you again, if you are interested. Maura."

She had enclosed her business card, which read, Maura Tobin, Personnel Manager, Smith Kline Clinical Laboratories, Inc. I was still alive and my imagination ran wild. I had my secretary hold my calls and I dialed Maura's office number. We chatted warmly and agreed to meet for dinner a week later. I made a reservation at Gaylord's in Ghirardelli Square. I have always loved Indian, it was my favorite, and Gaylord's offered San Francisco's finest. Buddha, a five-foot-tall statue, greeted guests as they entered. The walls were brushed in a faux gold finish. The room featured leather couches and embroidered throw pillows and ottomans. The tandoor, the source of the aromas and cuisine forged within it, was visible through a blue, tiled archway. Chefs laid roti and paratha onto its heated bricks. Ghee, curry and associated spices held the air fragrant. I was ten minutes into a Pimm's Cup at the bar when Maura arrived, not a minute before or after our agreed rendezvous. I stood.

Maura was nothing less than a model Renoir would have demanded sit for him. She was tall and thin and wore a scooped dress at once green and softened white. A black belt girded her narrow waist, matching her heels. She wore a strand of pearls and matching earrings. Her hair was caught in a bun. She was lovely and I was stunned. Our eyes met briefly. She looked right into me, a fragment of a moment now frozen in the warmth of time.

The hostess led us to our table beside a window that looked out over the bay. Conversation came easily, as did her smile. I lost, for that evening, all of my self doubt. She told me about her education—she had completed her undergraduate work in psychology at the University of California-Los Angeles and her master's in education at San Francisco State University. She told me about Mary, the cousin with whom she shared an apartment on Sacramento Street in The City. Maura loved art and theater and travel. She liked movies, sports and reading. I shared her interest in all that. On some things, we differed. She liked to snow ski. I did not. I enjoyed cooking. She didn't. Mary did and, as it turned out, was a true talent. Maura rode horses. I didn't. I gambled. She did not. I felt peaceful and at ease with her. And so our life together began, whether either of us truly knew it at the moment.

Our courtship lasted three years. Maura was thirty-one when we met. I was thirty-seven. We first traveled to New Orleans. I owned a cabin in Truckee, and we spent a weekend there most months, sometimes two. Maura taught me to snow ski. I taught her to cook. We read into the night by firelight. I met her family, and she got to know my son, Scott. Her many friends became mine. My few became hers. As 1981 gave way to 1982, I was as happy and fulfilled as I had ever been. Business was going well, and I had never dated anyone remotely like Maura. She was confident and had not a trace of arrogance. She was intelligent and listened intently. Whether or not my friend David had found his Fitzdare, Maura was mine.

As the calendar paged on and months and years yielded up jobs, challenges emerged. SmithKline downsized and Maura lost her job, among hundreds of others at the bloated company. Maura, as head of personnel, was assigned with terminating the others before she was assigned with terminating herself. Scott's adjustment to this idyll was less than ideal. He acted out. He threw tantrums, bringing tension to our relationship. Yet, Maura, who seemingly was equipped to handle any challenge, overcame that hurdle. She made it clear that she was willing to commit to a life together. I remained doubtful, cowardly. It took me fully another two years and four months before I realized I was a fool if I failed to heed her stated willingness to marry and build a family.

We never argued over my hesitation. In fact, we never argued about anything. Maura never pressed. And it made sense, at least to me, to hold off on marriage. We were busy. After Maura left SmithKline, she started her own company, The Personnel Bureau, which managed the intricacies of hiring and the exigencies of firing, for any number of small firms. Meanwhile, I was working up to fifteen hours a day. We were in love, we were building companies. What was the hurry? What was the harm in taking our time? Then the answers came.

Maura and I had by then been dating for two years. We were exclusive. At thirty three, Maura was concerned that her fertility clock was winding down. She wanted children and a husband to help raise them, yet I wouldn't commit. And then she went—in frustration? in anger?—on a date with another man.

Our friends Lisa and Eric had invited us on a weekend getaway to Yosemite, where they had rented a cabin. Maura accepted. I declined. She went alone—or so I presumed. I took Scott skiing at Lake Tahoe. Late Friday night, I called Maura, who didn't answer her phone. That was unusual. I called Mary, and asked if she had heard from Maura. She had.

"Miss Tobin's fine. I thought you knew, she went off for the weekend with Lisa, Eric, and Matt."

"Who the hell is Matt?"

"I think he's a friend of Eric's."

"What do you know about him?"

"I think he's a sales rep for Estee Lauder."

"Is he married?"

"No, I'm pretty sure he's single."

It hit me. Maura was on a date, a sleepover at that. I was being replaced. My what's-the-hurry argument suddenly revealed itself as sheer stupidity. I had, without thinking it through, encouraged her to look elsewhere.

My imagination shifted into overdrive. Lovely Miss Tobin was spending the weekend with another man. Probably a wealthy doctor, with whom she was snuggling contentedly in a romantic cabin in seductive Yosemite Valley. I saw him holding her as they gazed out a window at moonlight bouncing off the fresh snowpack. Above, stars twinkled like pearls, no! worse, like diamonds as large as the Ritz. I saw this sordid Dr. Matt and my beloved drinking hot rum before a kindled fireplace, him kissing her softly and her arms pulling him closer. I dialed Maura again, and then again, and again. No answer. It was only six-thirty in the early, flirtatious evening. Christ, were they already in bed?

I didn't sleep at all. Not twenty-four hours ago, Maura and I were young and fresh and bright and inseparable. My damnable insecurity washed ashore in drowning waves. Maura had given herself over to me and I was too stupid, too self-possessed to seize on that offer, on a generosity beyond anything anyone had ever before offered me. I had to see her. Scott and I left our cabin well before dawn Sunday morning and made our way to the interstate, which was slick beneath a mix of snow and freezing rain. Still, I attempted to make the typically three-hour drive back to San Francisco in two. Cellular reception was bad, and I pulled into a service station and dialed her on a payphone. No answer. I tried Mary's number. No answer. If Maura were avoiding my call, surely she wouldn't not pick up for her best friend, and it struck me then. I still considered Mary Maura's best friend. Why wasn't I? How could I have failed to become just that? I berated myself for being a horse's ass. I stopped again at a station and dropped quarters into a pay phone and dialed Mary again. This time she answered. It was six-thirty in the morning. I could tell I had woken her.

"Mary, it's Charles." I was nearly frantic. "Have you heard from Maura?"

"I think she's still in Yosemite with Lisa and Eric."

"And Matt," I said. By now, I had put him through medical school and through his rigorous residency, this genius neurosurgeon and handsome bastard who just so happened to dabble in cardiology, as well.

Mary was silent on the other end.

"Do you have any idea why she's not taking my calls? Would you call her for me? I can't reach her. Mary, will you tell her I love her?"

"I will, Charles, but I don't think you have anything to worry about."

"Thank you, Mary," I said, on the verge of tears. "Goodbye for now."

Radio reception can be lousy in the mountains and Scott was asleep on the backseat and so I was alone with my thoughts. How could I have allowed this to get to where it was? We loved one another. Was I just a fool? How could I save this?"

Green Ponderosa pine gave way to California Oak as we descended into the Sacramento Valley. The highway widened to four lanes even as my thinking further narrowed. I began imaging my next conversation with Maura.

"Scott and I had a lovely weekend. How was yours? Did you hit the slopes? Did you sleep with Matt."

I was lost in thought and barreling down the interstate on autopilot. I had neither seen nor heard the car behind me until a voice came from it over its loudspeaker: "Pull over!"

I did.

"May I see your driver's license?" The highway patrolman had stopped me a few miles west of Auburn after having clocked me at eighty-five miles an hour, twenty over the limit. I lied in a bid to talk my way out of a ticket: "I apologize, officer. I'm hurrying home to handle a family emergency."

He looked at me hard and then throughout the car. "Who's the little boy?"

"He's my son, sir." We looked at each other a long moment more and he issued me a warning and let me go. I dropped Scott off at his mother's home and drove to mine. Maura called shortly after three that afternoon.

I asked her, "Can you come by?"

She said yes and I thanked her and we hung up.

I had moved back to San Francisco in March 1983 to 7 Locust Street, in Pacific Heights. It was an elegant rental, from which I could see the Bay and Alcatraz anchored within it. My second-floor flat overlooked tree-lined Locust and Cherry streets. It boasted red oak floors and coffered ceilings and a wood-burning fireplace. I built a fire and put on a kettle to boil. Maura and I had spent many comfortable evenings there. The flat struck me as ideal for pro-posing marriage — and that's what I did that afternoon, albeit in an awkward way. I asked, "Would you like to change the address on your checks?"

"Are you crazy?"

"Yes, I am," I assured her, as goofy and nervous as a teenager. "I'm crazy about you. Will you marry me?"

She shook her head and then she said yes. I laughed my relief and kissed her and held her and she embraced me as well. I was as happy at that moment as I had ever been. We were engaged, bound by an agreement that specified no particular delivery date. I was fine with that; Maura was not, and her will ruled. We set a date.

Invitations went out to our families, and to three of my friends, and to thirty of Maura's dearest. Gaylord's catered the reception that incredible, magical day of September 15, 1984. We were married at our upper Haight-Ashbury home, at 1437 Cole Street. Maura's devoutly Catholic parents, Kathleen and Patrick, had wished that their elder daughter take her vows in the church, but Maura and I were, given the emerging allegations of priests' sexual abuse, opposed to the church sanctioning our marriage, and given that she and I were footing the bill for our wedding, there was no further discussion on the matter.

I have never been religious and have never had much faith in anything I hadn't gathered from direct experience. I had consulted with my business partner, Pierre, on secular nuptials; he and his wife, Sonja, had exchanged their vows on horseback in Golden Gate Park, a ceremony overseen by one Reverend Michael P. McDermott, who was licensed and nonsectarian and who worked out of a rented room on Tenth Avenue off Anza Street. He charged nothing, taking only what he termed cash tips. On the day of the wedding, the reverend arrived on his black Harley Davidson, an unlit cigarette dangling from the corner of his lips. The good reverend was a rotund yet otherwise tiny man and dressed in black. He was thus equally suited for overseeing weddings and funerals. He brought to mind a squashed Johnny Cash.

Thus we began our formally recognized union, one that conjoined conservative and liberal backgrounds. Maura was genteel. I was headstrong. It was an ideal marriage, one that overcame the varied challenges that can overwhelm lesser unions. I came to believe in a higher power, love.

THE EMBEZZLER

P acific Coast Plastics in July 1976 moved from the garage on Natoma Street into a twenty-three-thousand-five-hundred-square-foot building at 1235 Howard Street, which had been built in 1913 to house the San Francisco Fire Department's horses and the water rigs they pulled to this emergency and that. Later, the building housed a bakery. At one point, it served as a rehearsal studio for rock 'n' roll legends, including Jefferson Airplane. It was two stories tall with hardwood floors and hadn't been renovated in fifty years, but at a nickel a square foot, I had no complaint.

One rule of thumb in business is to avoid, if at all possible, doing something you either can't or don't understand. Often, those are the same. Normally, I adhered to my strategic plan. When instead I strayed into brainstorming, I found trouble, especially with personnel. I had no accounting savvy and needed someone who did.

Peter Burns was a con artist who by the time I hired him had embezzled hundreds of thousands of dollars from other small companies. Before learning this fact, I hired him to keep our books. He replaced Bookkeeper Bella, a referred friend of a friend. She had lasted two weeks, during which she went through a case of unsharpened pencils. She recorded ledger entries with the first of the case and wore down the erasers of the other nineteen. I had no choice but to let her go and ran an ad in the San Francisco Chronicle seeking her replacement. And so it was that Mr. Peter Burns joined Pacific Coast Plastics.

Had I turned to Central Casting, I couldn't have found a bookkeeper with a more quintessential appearance. He wore glasses and dressed conservatively in a worn, blue suit. He holstered pens and pencils in a plastic shirt pocket protector. He appeared frail and thin, nearly malnourished. He had a slightly humped back and a quiet manner. His résumé was flawless. It was structured and devoid of spelling or grammar errors. He had worked for well-known companies and moved from one to another without a lapse.

Everybody liked Peter, without knowing just why. My personnel manager called his contacts and reported back that Burns was "good as gold." My accountant and banker similarly were impressed. I brought him on board, relieved to have filled such a key position with such a sterling prospect. Not ninety days later, the company was on the verge of bankruptcy.

One Monday morning during Peter's third month on the job, he failed to show up. The company's check register lay on his desk. The last check, No. 1446, was made out to one George Smith. There was no reference to its amount. Without exactly knowing it was the case, I knew we had been embezzled. George Smith was a fictitious name. So, too, was Peter Burns.

"Burns" and his team had worked their scam again. A clerk in our personnel department in vetting him had dialed the phone numbers he had provided rather than turning to directory assistance. Rather than reaching IBM's personnel department, she had spoken with Burn's co-conspirators. They assured her he was top notch. They had been sorry to see him go.

I had spent the past several years building the company on which I and my genuine employees depended for our livelihoods. Peter Burns had fractured that with all the concern for others of a sociopath. We began receiving past-due accounts from suppliers. Peter Burns through some sort of accounting legerdemain had drained the company, which now had sizeable debt and no cash, while our financial statements showed glowing, twenty percent profit margins. By then, we had heard from vendors demanding payment. I was at a loss; there were no inventory shortages and my company's bank account balanced. We owed Cyro Industries, our main supplier of raw plastic, more than forty thousand dollars. As we dug deeper, we found that we were in arrears with every one of our vendors. The guy was good.

Peter was still on my payroll and suggested that we factor our receivables until the issue was resolved. I refused. Instead, I cut expenses, froze wages and gave employees time off instead of bonuses, without telling them what had happened.

Later I learned that we had been taken for sixty-eight thousand dollars, and by then Burns had vanished. He had been cutting checks to a third party who cashed them. He had posted ledger entries to our suppliers in the check register to offset the credits.

The San Francisco Police Department's Fraud Division took a report and created a sketch of the vanished Burns. They filed away their copy. I took mine and went in search of him. No one working the front desks in nearby hotels or restaurants recognized him. I sought to track him down through his utility bills. I contacted Pacific Gas & Electric, pretending to be him, but to no avail. Burns had once mentioned that he had earned master points in bridge. I dropped in on a sanctioned bridge tournament in Oakland. There was no one named Burns among the two hundred participants. Eventually, I was glad I had failed to find him. What I would have done to him was a felony.

I called the FBI, and I wasn't the first to have done so. They were looking for him. "Peter Burns," a special agent told me, was an ex-con who specialized in forgery, embezzlement, and disguises, explaining why no one recognized him from the police sketch. Moreover, he was addicted to cocaine. He was the front man for a four- or five-person gang. Two were operating from prison. The bunch had hit several companies up and down California. One business owner suffered a heart attack on discovering he had been taken for two-hundred-thousand dollars.

One morning, while "Peter Burns" was eating breakfast at a Denny's in San Diego, an FBI special agent approached and placed him under arrest. The agent later testified that Burns had demonstrated no remorse. He only wanted to know, "How did you find me?" He was tried and convicted and sent to prison.

My relationship with Cyro Industries survived the affair, debunking the idea that large companies have no heart. Our company owed more than we could immediately pay to resolve our debt, Cyro could have stopped shipping plastic to us and lined up with other vendors hoping at least to receive pennies on the dollar for what we owed had we been forced to file for bankruptcy protection. Instead they could keep working with us, trusting in our future and our ability to make them whole. I met with Cyro executives we had worked with, and though my earlier demands had earned me the joking sobriquet of Prince Charles—apparently acceptable behavior given that we had always paid our invoices on time prior to the "Peter Burns" affair. Cyro gave us the break that saved our company. We shook hands and went back to work.

Pacific Coast Plastics became one of Cyro's leading distributors. Eventually, I was asked to join its National Distributor Advisory Committee. We had survived the embezzlement and I learned from the experience. I almost—almost—thank the con man who came so close to ruining us.

CHARACTERS

Hiring people is always, and always will be, something of a crapshoot. We hired any number of ambitious, and detail-oriented people. We also hired our share of ambitious, detail-oriented mistakes. All told, the payroll over time boasted people who helped develop the company, some of whom were clear-eyed, others whose eyes were dilated but their contributions nevertheless significant. The fifty-year-old bookkeeper we hired to replace Peter Burns checked out — we had learned among other things how better to vet potential hires — wore a coat and tie to his interview. Yet he showed up his first day dressed in leather and chains. By the end of week two, he came to the office in motorcycle boots, a silver-studded, black hat with a holstered cap pistol along his thigh. I admired his faith in his appearance, yet the day after his ninety-day probationary period ended and his company-paid insurance kicked in, Frank claimed to suffer from pyria and scurvy and had his teeth removed. Our insurance carrier denied his claim and he left.

Lovely, long-legged, redheaded Jenna replaced him. Jenna was a fine bookkeeper and apparently an equally fine bedfellow. She slept with at least three colleagues and eventually married a buyer from Macy's.

And then there was Bryan Courtney, part Walter Mitty, part WC Fields, and a dash of Elmer Gantry all in one. He was a misanthrope liked by everyone. He was forty-five years old when he came on board and, not coincidentally, was the best salesman I have ever met. He expressed a lofty ambition of leading the company into the Fortune 500 listings. He was heavyset and had a bulbous nose prominent on a flushed white face. Bryan worked on the order desk. No telling what he would have accomplished with just a shred of self-discipline. As it was, his love of booze, women, and gambling sabotaged any such success.

I had never—and never have since—met anyone remotely like Bryan. In his man-of-the-world way, he was quite impressive: he could identify single-malt scotch by its aroma, talk the clothes off a nun, and sell plastic for two times its market value. He memorized our employee handbook, and much of the sixty-page product catalog, within weeks. Bryan flipped his charm switch and seduced customers. Buyers loved his delivery, which was a blend of knowledge and advice, sprinkled with dashes of humor. He skillfully juggled words like so many balls, delighting buyers with his spontaneous jocularity. Bryan loved the hustle. His sales skills were impressive yet were inconsistent with our business plan, which was conservative and predictable. Our products were not unique. Where we excelled was in offering great service. We sold our materials at Volvo prices; Bryan sold at Ferrari prices. That was unsustainable. His short-term, high-margin hustles defied our company's practices. On one hand, he was formidable with his imagination and magnificent gift of gab. On the other, he was doomed to fail.

Cancerous growths demand ever-greater amounts of nourishment. Gambling was Bryan's insatiable cancer. Money sticks to some fingers and slips through others. Bryan was the sort of gambler who did well in the interim, and went broke in the end. Earlier in his career, he had calculated odds for The Gold Sheet, a betting and sports information newsletter. He bet on sports some, but his primary game was single-deck blackjack—he was adroit at counting cards.

Bryan's sharp, unrestrained humor and free thinking appealed to me. I shared—to a degree—some of his weaknesses; I, too, liked a bet and a bottle of fine wine, but I possessed control alien to his, particularly given that his was non-existent. Several weeks into the job, Bryan landed a significant account and came to me with a request.

"I told you I could make you money, Charles. And you now know I was right."

"You did, Bryan, and yes you are. Good work."

"I've got an idea. How about a trip to Las Vegas. We'll have a great time."

"Who's we?"

"You and me. I'd like an advance in the form of a round-trip ticket to Vegas, and I want you to come with me. I'll pay you back from my winnings."

More out of curiosity than anything else, a chance to gain a better understanding of my employee, I went along with it. We caught a flight that Friday morning. By mid-afternoon, we were golfing at the Tropicana with rented clubs against a couple of Vegas sharps. Bryan had arranged the match at $50 a man per hole. At the turn, we each were out $350, and we dropped out. Bryan had set us up with adjoining top-floor suites at the Landmark. I was impressed because this happened to be the final weekend of March Madness, when whatever rooms might still be available went at a premium. Bryan, or at least so he said, had managed to arrange them comp. After our half round of golf, I saw Bryan only twice more the rest of the weekend after leaving him after dinner that first night at a single-deck blackjack table. He was still there at eight the next morning, sitting behind a stack of black chips a foot high.

"Why don't your give me three of those chips to cover your airfare."

"That would be bad luck, Charles. No can do."

The next time I saw him, two hours before our Monday morning flight, Bryan showed up at the hotel. My employee had played blackjack and placed a bet or two at the sports book, nonstop for two days and nights. His only interruption, he told me, was a dalliance with a couple of hookers Sunday morning. He hadn't slept since we arrived, and he had lost everything he had won. That I found out when he hit me up for breakfast. His problem was now obvious, and though he asked from time to time, I never accompanied him anywhere again. He continued to do well the job I had hired him for. Two months later, however, I came to realize just how sick Bryan was.

Bryan asked for permission to come in an hour late one midweek workday. The following morning, he came into my office and pulled a roll of hundred-dollar bills from his right pants pocket and a matching sum from his left. He said he had made twelve-thousand dollars playing cards. He was beaming. Late that night, He called me collect from Reno, asking for bus fare home. He had lost his entire stake.

Bryan claimed that he had once played pool against Willie Mosconi. Testing his account, I suggested we shoot a few games of eight-ball. Playing well, I sank four or five balls in a row. Bryan ran the table twice in a row while downing shots of Jack Daniel's.

Two friends of mine, Erick Steinberg and Richard Hoffman, one morning joined Bryan and me for a round of golf at Peacock Gap Golf Club in San Rafael. Bryan made a hole in one on the par-three sixth hole. He seemed unimpressed with the rarity. Most golfers would have kept the ball as a keepsake, maybe even framed it, but not Bryan. On the next hole he sliced the trophy out of bounds onto the adjacent driving range.

It was around that time that Jenna, our lovely, long-legged, red-headed bookkeeper, decided she was in love with unlovely, short-legged, bald Bryan—and moved in with him. For one reason or another, he confided in her, confessing that Bryan Courtney was an alias and that he had jumped bail while on probation for an income-tax conviction. Heartbroken, Jenna told me the morning Bryan skipped town. Maura took over as Pacific Coast Plastics' personnel manager. She brought professionalism to the post, implementing better screening, and we began to land more stable employees. I had been responsible for hiring and tended to be taken by personalities rather than by more useful traits. If an applicant had struck me as bright, or fun, or had a sense of humor, I tended to bring him or her on board—typically to the company's detriment. I can be a slow learner. Maura was anything but.

THE EARTHQUAKE

During the summer of 1987, Pacific Coast Plastics reduced staff and space. We moved into a building on Folsom Street between Eighth and Ninth streets. Two years later, we merged with a similarly small company known as Architectural Plastics. The deal closed in October. I brought to the new company a large customer base and solid suppliers. Architectural's owner, Lamont Pierre Miremont, brought fabrication skills and deep pockets. We bought a building in Petaluma even though I still had a year and a half left on my lease on 865 Folsom Street. October 17 had become my magic date. It was my mother's birthday, and the day of my career-building sale of chair mats to Continental Oil in New York—and best of all, I had met Maura on the seventeenth of October.

On October 17, 1989, tectonic plates deep beneath the Bay Area shifted violently, triggering the Loma Prieta earthquake. The massive tremor, coming as the San Francisco Giants were minutes away from hosting the Oakland A's in the World Series, dropped a section of the Bay Bridge, killed dozens, and destroyed thousands of houses and buildings, including that at 865 Folsom Street. That week, I received a letter from my company's attorney, James Bow. It read "Dear Charles: When you said earlier this year that you would move heaven and earth to get out of your Folsom Street lease, you apparently weren't kidding. The rent is to be prorated as of October 17. You should get back a refund of $1,431 of the October rent. The security deposit of $2,650 as well should be fully refunded to you."

Pierre and I that evening had gone out to dinner and through a window forty miles north of the devastation watched smoke blacken the sky over San Francisco. All bridges into the city were closed.

Three days later, when the Golden Gate Bridge reopened I crossed into San Francisco to inspect our building. A trench ran through the entire structure. The building was tagged for demolition.

Pierre and I worked another six years together. I sold my interest in the company to him, and we went our separate ways. After selling plastic for nineteen years, I was burned out. Still, I started a new company, Sonoma Graphic Products, and eventually dabbled in commercial real estate before retiring in 2003.

DEVASTATION

With fewer competing demands on our time, Maura and I blossomed as a couple as the enjoyment we derived from one another grew, and as we grew older we grew even closer. Alexandra, our first daughter, was born on January 26, 1986. Nearly three years later, on November 13, 1988, our second daughter, Lauren, was born. Six years later, we moved into a charming house on Sawgrass Place in Santa Rosa, where we enjoyed nine blissful years before tragedy struck.

I had begun in 2002 to suspect that Maura was suffering some undetermined illness. Previously gregarious and friendly, she had become reserved, reclusive even. She became temperamental when facing even the slightest problem. Our family was on the verge of a challenge none of us could have, or would have, imagined. Several of Maura's girlfriends had noticed the same changes. Soon enough, Maura began to lose weight and had become forgetful. My concern was now beyond suspicion. One evening, Mary arrived for dinner at Maura's invitation. Maura had forgotten to shop. Over time, she began to slur her speech as the day wore on; by late afternoon she sounded drunk. By evening, I couldn't understand a word she said. My wife, a woman with a master's degree in psychology, couldn't put a complete sentence together. In social settings, she rarely spoke. Her attempts to communicate had become gestures that no one understood.

Late that year, doctors diagnosed Maura with Bulbar Amyotrophic Lateral Sclerosis, a subtly progressive and ultimately fatal disorder of the nervous system. ALS attacks nerve cells and neural pathways to the brain and spinal cord, causing the body's motor neurons to waste away. Speaking, swallowing and breathing become progressively all but impossible.

There is no cure. Few live more than five years after such a diagnosis. The great Yankee outfielder Lou Gehrig's death from ALS gave it its eponymous, shorthand descriptor, Lou Gehrig's disease. It, like all disease, is indiscriminate. It has laid waste to senators, in Jacob Javits; to actors, in David Niven; and to perfect mothers and wives, in our Maura.

The girls and I were devastated. It was as though the gates of hell had swung open. My thoughts were as uncontrollable as sparklers, my mind effusively turning between wishes to make her days as comfortable as I could and the inevitability of life without her—the latter thought hurt beyond words—without the woman whom I loved so deeply and who still slept beside me as she further slipped away. Maura seemed oblivious to the fact that she was dying. Somehow, despite her pain, she seemed relatively happy as the accompanying dementia took over her. She had no idea that in all likelihood she would choke to death. I hated the literature about the disease that I nevertheless read as though somewhere within it I might find an explanation of how this horror was even possible. Maura's diet now was restricted to liquid aliment, although she on more than one occasion came across and tried to swallow solid food. The children and I, as a result, learned the Heimlich maneuver.

As her mind further deteriorated, I child-proofed the house. Toxic substances were removed. The gas stove was disconnected. House keys were hidden. A pick tube eventually was inserted into her stomach, the only way the girls and I could feed her. On trips outside the house as we attempted to maintain some semblance of normalcy, Maura's inevitable coughing spells, her body's desperate attempts to clear her essential air passage, discomfited strangers. Her voice was reduced to a whisper. People's discomfort with her condition angered me, although I supposed were I in their seats I might have felt the same. Our daughters were traumatized, and with Maura's downturn, they, too, declined. They began withdrawing from their mother. Coming into adolescence, they needed a mother's guidance, but that was no longer possible. Fourteen-year-old Lauren and sixteen-year-old Alexandra stopped asking Maura for answers as her responses became ever more incoherent. Each reacted in her own way.

Lauren internalized her feelings, keeping her thoughts largely to herself. She wrote: "My response to my mother's death directly reflects my temperament. Instead of vocalizing my feelings, I chose to store them deep in the recesses of my brain. I resisted the help of counselors and chose not to discuss the issue unless it was necessary. I internalized the pain because it bothered me when people knew I was hurting. I preferred to be quietly independent."

Alex acted out, seeking some form of solace in alcohol and drugs. I sent her off to her aunt's home, in Moorpark, some five hundred miles away, and paid for her to enter counseling. I was losing my wife, and now one of my two precious daughters was gone.

The death of a parent removes an essential half of a child's world, leaving her in a place that was no longer as safe as it had been. I found myself in the same, insecure world.

As Maura and I drove home from the University of California at San Francisco the day her condition was diagnosed, crossing north on the Golden Gate Bridge toward Santa Rosa, I lied to her, turning to her and saying, "I think the test results are favorable, sweetheart. If they come back otherwise, would you want me to share that with you?"

She looked at me with tear-filled eyes, unable to talk, and shook her head no. I looked back at the road ahead and held back my own tears.

I honored Maura's wish, and I don't believe she ever knew she was terminally ill. I told only our most trusted and beloved friends. I kept Maura's fate a secret from her elderly parents until near the end.

Maura's illness did have a silver lining, one that involved my friendship with my childhood friend Michael. My relationship with Maura had begun the night when Michael and I met her and Mary at Prego's and Michael had made all of us laugh when after she asked if he had a card he had thrown his Visa on the table. Like most male friends, Michael and I rarely shared the intimacies of our private lives. That changed when Maura became ill. He and I then spoke every week. He referred me to healthcare providers he knew to be competent. He knew when to sprinkle a dash of humor into our conversation. His friendship became a lifeline.

In late June, Maura lapsed into an irreversible coma. Hospice nurses, as gently as such news could be delivered, advised me that she likely had no more than ten days left. I had to choose whether we would spend them at home or in a medical setting. I never discussed it with Alex or Lauren. I didn't know how. The question, "Well, girls, where do you want your mother's life to end?" wasn't one I could ask. I made the decision that my beloved Maura should spend her final days in the home she and the girls and I loved— and where we had spent nine wondrous years before we received her shattering diagnosis. The decision to remove Maura's feeding tube was the most difficult of my life. I felt guilty and sad beyond any words, only the deep-throated sobbing that gave way to my anguished bawling got me through it—if it ever has. On July 6, 2003, Maura Tobin Levine died peacefully at home in the company of her family and her friends.

Yet, Maura in one sense never left. Her kindness and presence remain with me. Her unheard voice continues to guide me.

Yet, her absence affected how I moved on, now a father without a wife to smooth the rough edges of parenting. I distanced myself emotionally and made decisions about the children—and about my own life and needs—as though a spectator. Many of my decisions proved beneficial; others did not. Shortly after Maura's death, I retired. The company I had founded, after Pierre bought me out, Sonoma Graphic Products, resold digital imaging equipment, printing film, and plastics. It did well, and we plowed the profits into a parcel of land on which we built two concrete, tilt-up buildings. One housed our company, the other we rented out. Maura was in charge of personnel. I entered into negotiations in June 2002 to sell the company, a deal that closed a year later, two weeks after Maura left us. Now, I was our children's only parent. Maura had overseen hiring and all that that entailed and had run our household. I soon would find myself challenged by only the latter half of that burden. My appreciation of my late wife only grew.

AFTER MAURA

With Maura's death and the sale of the company, I inherited an emptied world. There was no doubt about the quelling impact of both. Maura was the driving spirit in my life. My professional success was chaperoned by a quiet, domesticated life, centered around her and family. No longer would I hear, "I'm so happy you're home, dear. The kids and I prepared something special for dinner," or the loving jab, "It's only Saturday. Why are you home so early? Is the business in trouble?"

Maura and I had progressed along our conjoined path. Now, she was gone.

The daunting difficulties of assuming dual parenthood and finding work to fill some of my other time were depressive. I often wondered when, or even if, I would ever hear Alex and Lauren laugh again. Recovery was slow, an emotional paralysis. I lived in Santa Rosa another seven years.

I became a man of deeper reflection. By the end of the first year, I had grown more than any previous year. Raising the girls kept me busy until Lauren left for college a few years later. I also returned to school, first at Santa Rosa Junior College, before completing my bachelor's degree at Dominican University. I undertook graduate work at Stanford. Memories of Maura's debilitation began to fade; the countless better memories filling that void. I began to feel comfortable again.

Golf and academia provided new friends and acquaintances. Still, I was detached. I spent evenings alone. My thoughts drifted to earlier days. Mannheim memories occasionally surfaced. One night I decided to seek out my old army buddy, David. Thirty-five years had passed since I had last seen him. Still, his indelible mark lingered in my mind. Few people had ever made a greater impression. I searched for him on the internet December 2009. The initial inquiry was futile. Nothing appeared using his full name, David Cameron Craver. Nor, did anything come up under those of his sisters, Janet and Cicely. David spoke often about living in Great Britain. I checked websites in London. Two days into the search I found him. It was too late. His obituary had appeared in a London publication. He had died on Friday, November 27, 2009, just days before I began my search.

A few condolences were attached to the obit. One was from a woman named Vicky, who I assumed was his wife. I began looking for Vicky Craver—and I attempted to reach out to John Riley, the obituary's author.

I found neither. The mortuary that had handled David's arrangements didn't respond to calls. Companies he had worked for weren't willing to discuss a former employee or his family.

At a roadblock, every effort having failed, I dropped the project for the next three years.

The exercise, however, stimulated my curiosity—I had become curious as to whether David had found his perfect mate as I had—and I began to seek, if not another Maura, at least someone to embrace and spend time with.

PARI, THE MATCHMAKER

N ewcomers, lonely men, newly moneyed men, heartbroken
widowers throughout San Francisco's history have found
company through the offices of women available for a price—and
from those inclined to make matches. Lillie Hitchcock Coit smoked
cigars, gambled and loved firemen. Sally Stanford ran an elegant
brothel on Nob Hill. Pauline Phillips advised the forlorn as Dear
Abby. Pari Livermore brought together hundreds of eligible men
and women by hosting parties, whose singles guests often heard
the same kind of music, those great symphonies of possibilities that
ultimately went nowhere. She also raised millions for charities. By
the time I met Pari, my sense of loss in Maura's absence had come
to overwhelm me. Pari introduced me to any number of attractive, bright, and sophisticated women—none of whom proved an
ideal match.

I took many of them out—some repeatedly—for five or six
years before I met a brilliant, engaging, often delightful, occasionally maddening physician, thanks to Pari. Sue and I agreed to meet
for an early evening cocktail at Harris Restaurant in San Francisco
and ended up talking for hours. We dated for the next several years.
Sue lived in Hillsborough and worked in San Francisco. I had
recently moved from my former home with Maura in Santa Rosa
to a fifteenth-floor, downtown apartment in The City. Sue and I
were drawn to one another, though our temperaments were anything but alike.

Love doesn't move in a straight line, it zig zags. But that was
not much consolation. I thought the relationship would work. It
did not. Our synthesis had the lure and pizzazz of excitement, yet
was foiled by the hindrance of uncertainty. Nine times we called it
off; eight times we came back together. We were living in a bizarre

state of romantic purgatory, never achieving the love necessary to enter the joy of a permanent union. Pari at one point said that if a relationship wasn't going to work, there was nothing anyone could do to make it work; if it were to work, nothing could stop it. She knew of what she spoke.

I knew it had to end, it was as clear as glass, but was clueless as to how to accomplish a clean break. It was then that I recounted my childhood friend Michael's gentle advice: "Never break off a relationship, untie it." Ultimately, I heeded his words. The parting was cordial, and Sue and I talked less and less until we both moved on. In May of 2013, I headed to Europe, and the ending was complete.

FINDING VICKY

I spent four months in the Old World with the fondness of a romantic, and the sadness of a lonely man. I enjoyed virtually everything I saw, heard, touched, smelled, and tasted—all of that alone. I gadded about, eventually winding up where my trip had begun, in London. I had ten days left before my ticket home expired. I spend much of those days in the determined guise of a diligent if less than adept detective, intent on finding David Craver's widow, Vicky. My efforts revolved not around thoughts of romance or of companionship, but rather on how David's life had evolved. I realized, too, to an extent, I was looking for something about myself.

I had come across David's obituary on a former employer's website, that of Computer Weekly, where my friend had served as editor from 1982 until 1990. He had suffered a heart attack while in France six months before he died.

"David's years were heady ones," Riley, his former colleague, had written, "and under his charismatic leadership Computer Weekly constantly broke new ground, overtook the opposition and moved into a new league of journalism. ... David had a sparkling personality full of drive, enthusiasm and humor, and a deep sense of humanity. He was a strong editor, being an inspirational leader, outstanding people-person and team builder. He was exceptionally good at nurturing upcoming journalists, and many of his appointments are scattered around the national media today. He empowered his staff and also shielded them from any unwarranted external pressure or nonsense from industry or upstairs."

According to the obituary, David was an excellent tennis player and decent on the squash court. He had moved on to launch UK operations at the publishing house of Ziff Davis, where he ultimately rose to become the company's managing director and senior vice president for Europe, until VNU, a Dutch publisher, bought the company in July 2000.

"We send our condolences to his wife Vicky, who supported him strongly during his time at Computer Weekly, and to his family," Riley concluded.

I had known nothing of his career. The photo that accompanied the heartfelt article erased any doubt I may have had as to whether this was the same man I had known and had relied on so many years past. I was determined to find Vicky.

I phoned Computer Weekly and was transferred to personnel, where a manager recalled Riley, who was no longer with the company, and found his contact information. He agreed to forward a message to Riley if I put my request in writing.

I wrote: "Dear John: David Craver and I were best friends while in the U.S. Army. Upon my discharge in 1969, I stayed with David's family in New Jersey before moving to New York. I moved to California in 1974 and I lost track of David after that, other than a few phone conversations. In December 2009, I learned of his passing through the obituary you posted online. I was utterly dismayed by the news. David was one of the most inspirational persons I ever met. I regret not having contacted him before his death. I'd like to tell his early story to Vicky, whom I have never met. But only if she wants to hear it. I have only good thoughts and words to express. I am a widower. My wife of nineteen years passed away, leaving behind myself and two young daughters to raise. I understand love lost. I come to you with this request because I believe it is the right thing to do. I feel confident David would approve, and assume his widow would appreciate the information about her husband. ... I will be in London until September 16."

I gave him my cell number, and Vicky called within the hour. We set a time to meet for coffee the next day.

SERENDIPITY

Good fortune comes in streaks. I once popped up three consecutive bloopers, each of which somehow managed to fall behind the shortstop for a Texas league single. Likewise, each stop of my twelve-nation European trip brought fortune—of a more serendipitous nature. The windmills of Holland demonstrated that man can, at times, harness nature. The Dutch metaphorically believe the milling blades represent life propelled by the spirit of the divine. Architectural wonders, such as the Colosseum in Rome, inspire awe and justify words ending in "-est." French cassoulet and Catalan paella evidenced a different genius. Mona Lisa transfixed me. And now I had found Vicky, the culmination of a search that I had begun to doubt possible; I hoped she would find value in my memories of her late husband, and that, perhaps, I could learn something further about him—and myself.

David had helped me survive a regimentation I never could have taken to and led me to a career, and, too, he had helped Vicky begin a family. I suspected this final stop—England, the thirteenth nation on my itinerary—might provide an enlightening trip with a great ending.

The first thing I learned about Vicky was that she had excellent taste. She chose for us to meet at the 1921 art deco Wolseley, Taste of London's restaurant of the decade. I passed through a revolving brass door between marble archways into a room walled in polished stone quarried from Dorset's Isle of Portland, and blue York dressings. The floor was laid in intricately patterned, black-and-white marble. Black, lacquered Doric columns rose to the domed ceiling. Polished brass and etched glass glinted all about. Tuxedoed waiters were as polished as their speech and dress. This was going to be an expensive cup of coffee.

I arrived fifteen minutes early and was ushered to a window seat overlooking Piccadilly. Questions rippled through my mind: Had David ever mentioned my name? Would I find Vicky interesting, receptive, open? Would any such possible attraction prove mutual? I have no idea why I had constructed this odd mental architecture that allowed me to fleetingly raise Vicky to goddess statue. I had, of course, never met her, nor had I even ever seen a photograph of her.

I worked to calm myself. For all I knew, Vicky might have been an ax murderess—or, I couldn't resist the thought—the very personification of Donleavy's Fitzdare. David, now forty or more years ago—while he and I were still in our early twenties—had sought just such a woman, a perfect wife, balanced and complex, with an earthy quality. I realized I had now turned Vicky from a human being into a perfect wine. I began to realize that if she didn't soon show, I might teeter on the edge of imaginative insanity. I felt with great conviction that I desperately needed a martini to settle me down. But that likely might raise an eyebrow on her imagined perfect face. I passed on the notion. We were meeting, after all, for coffee.

Looking about, I saw a woman come through the revolving door and knew, through some instinct, that she was my friend's widow. Somehow, too, she seemed to recognize me and walked briskly to where I was sitting until I stood to introduce myself. Vicky was a very English woman in a very English setting. She had on ironed jeans above black riding boots and below a grey sweater, and wore a Burberry raincoat. She brushed aside a stray fringe of blonde hair and took my hand. I felt a wave of relief. Vicky was petite and exuded a youthful manner, far younger than her sixty some years. We mutually suggested something stronger than coffee, and she ordered champagne and I the martini I no longer felt was so necessary, but nevertheless was relaxing.

Vicky asked, "Have you ever before been to London?"

"Yes," I said. "I marched in Trafalgar Square, protesting the American War."

"Which war?"

"The one in Southeast Asia."

"That was the Vietnam War," she corrected me.

"The Vietnamese would beg to differ."

She laughed.

"I have been excited to connect with an old friend of David's about whom I had heard a good deal," she said.

"He was a wonderful friend," I said. She smiled and nodded.

I told her about his and my time in Mannheim and how I had come to rely on his intellect and gentle nature. She told me how David and she had come to meet; she had been visiting New York. The evening they met, as it turned out, was the last time I ever saw him.

She had told me apologetically that she had only two hours before a subsequent appointment, and those one hundred and twenty minutes passed in a blink. As she stood to leave, Vicky invited me to visit her in Lewes. I took her up on it a few days later.

The village of Lewes, in the county of East Sussex, lies some forty-four miles south of London and is home to nineteen thousand people. It is the birthplace of the writer and political activist Thomas Paine, who, like so many others from the isles, migrated to America. Vicky lived alone on High Street in a home known as Trevor House. She had been twenty-two and David thirty-one when they married in 1981. He took a job in London, and she taught English Literature at Brighton University. She still does. Life treated them well until it dealt a harsh blow to their charmed time together. I could empathize. They had purchased Trevor House in 1993, one hundred and seventy three years after it was build close to the one thousand-year-old Norman Castle. They did well—David in particular had been well compensated—and they took title to a second home, La Petite Bargide, in Visan, France. In the spring of 2009, however, David suffered cardiac arrest while cycling in the countryside outside Visan. He was medically evacuated back to England after two weeks during which he lay in a coma in a hospital in Avignon. His prognosis went from bad to worse, and four months later he was moved to a nursing home where he spent the final few weeks of his life. The home originally had been built inside a military base. It was the only facility available that boasted the specialists and equipment to deal with his extreme circumstances. "Imagine that," Vicky told me, appreciative of the irony, "what an ending for a conscientious objector."

Our conversations that week carried late into the night, typically following dinner with her friends and family. I met their children: Dominic, Daisy, and Lily. They, too, wanted to know what I could share about their father's past. I wanted to know about his career.

One evening, I asked Vicky to describe David as husband and father.

"I would say he was an articulate and idealistic dreamer. He was witty, fun, and had a great sense of the absurd. He was a wonderful storyteller."

I asked her to relate one. She excused herself and minutes passed before she returned with a hefty manuscript, which she laid on the table between us.

"David made a lot of money as a Ziff Davis executive. He worked long hours, but hated the job. He wanted to stay home and write. That's what he did in his retirement. This is what he wrote. I'd like to discuss it with you after you've read it."

She left me alone with David's work, which, too, was a memoir, albeit written in the third person, an authorial decision I didn't quite understand. Much of his recounting chronicled his family, past and present. I was surprised and pleased to discover I appeared in it, as well.

I began reading his account that evening sitting in the very chair in which he had composed it. The room faced west over a sprawling garden that gave way to the Lewes countryside through French doors. When I periodically looked out, starlings looked back. The walls were painted ruby red and decorated with African art and framed oils and abstract watercolors.

I picked up the next afternoon where I had left off and into the evening. A short time into the work, a peculiar sensation came over me, an awareness of something present in the room more substantial than the pervasive silence. David was returning to life. I felt I was being watched as I read. The purpose of my visit to Lewes was to tell Vicky of her husband's past. Now, I was learning about myself from the words of a dead man. His words were great because they portrayed me in a strikingly new way, an experience that I had never had before. As I read on, my old habits of self-perception and imagination altered. I began to understand what Fredrick Douglas meant when he said "It's easier to build strong children than to repair broken men." Continuing, I knew my 68-year-old world was about to change, 'to repair' if you will, and inarguably, become more vibrant and filled with greater joy.

In Mannheim, David and I occupied opposite posts. He was one step below an officer. I was one above a sad sack. I felt inferior to him, put always a bit off balance by his social status, intelligence, and self assuredness. Sitting in his chair, now, leaning back, I discovered that I similarly had had an influence on him. "He would go out most evenings, alone or with friends, although most did not have the determination to get off base as often as he did," he wrote of himself in that oddly chosen third person. "Sometimes his new soul mate, Charles Levine, would go with him, but too often he was pulling extra duty or had been confined to the barracks for yet another indiscretion he had committed against the sanctity of the army's rules, regulations and sensitivities. He and Charles, or sometimes, Chuck, had met when David moved back into barracks with his new job, a brigade clerk. Chuck hated the silly, bullying, soulless, regimented, impersonal routines as much as David, but while David internalized his anger, Chuck let it all hang out and ran into trouble almost on a daily basis. Much as David admired his bolshiness, it was difficult to describe his strategy as very effective. Chuck grew up in California where he had honed his skills as a baseball player and claimed to have had a shot at the major leagues. ...

"When David met Charles he was one year into his term and still a buck private. Every time he earned a private's stripe ... he would be busted for yet another confrontation with someone in authority. So here was this tall, gangling, black-haired handsome guy spending most of his days and nights in wrinkled fatigues pulling guard duty or KP—kitchen patrol—as it was so oddly called.

"Still, he did manage to get away now and again, and then they shared their thoughts and consoled one another over many a fine stein of lager."

I put down the memoir, leaned back against the headrest, and reconsidered its author. David was the first person from the upper-middle class who had ever befriended me. He came from the New York area, a place I had dreamed of living in from childhood. He was well-mannered, and got along with everyone. He seemed much different than me, but I discovered we shared a mutual sense of insecurity. I continued to read on. David wrote of himself, "He was intelligent, everyone said so. And while in truth he didn't understand what he did to deserve the praise, its constant reaffirmation was necessary to maintain confidence. One sloughs off the flatterers, but let the flatterer desist and one sulks in silence."

I was flattered that he had considered me—that he respected me—a soul mate of sorts. I had assumed he was the better man because of his better background and education. His memoir, however, confirmed that where you stand determines what you see. We may see the same accident, or hear the same words, but don't interpret either in exactly the same way. David and I came from opposite sides of the tracks and thus viewed life differently. After forty years, reading his thoughts changed how I viewed him, and revealed how unfairly I had perceived myself.

Vicky and I met for tea the next morning. I thanked her for showing me the memoir and confessed that I was somewhat ill at ease reading about David's and her life together. Yet, as I read further into the work, I realized I wanted in on the whole story, from beginning to end.

I told her that what David had written convinced me I had undersold myself. Vicky laughed and told me that so, too, had David, and perhaps for that reason, he told her, he had failed to close the deal with Patrizia. Moreover, Vicky told me, that his transfer from the gunner program to the clerical position was a fluke. David's mother, Vicky said, chatted up everyone, including someone in line at a Jersey market who it turned out was a Spec-4 army clerk, who happened to work in the records department at Fort Dix. Her new friend subsequently changed David's orders as an unsolicited favor. Nor, Vicky told me, were David's parents the rich, East Coast bluebloods that I had presumed. In fact, they scraped by. He had relied on my friendship, as I had his, to get by in a place and institution neither of us would ever have chosen. I now knew as Vicky and I talked that David and I had far more in common than I had realized—although, of course, he was better educated though I doubt he had much in the way of an arm.

I told her that while stationed in Mannheim, I was a guy feeling his way in a new world I couldn't fathom and so lacked confidence in myself. I told her how much I had admired and been intimidated by David's erudition and suavity, and then she surprised me.

"The impression David always gave me of you was that you were a lady's man. You came across to him as a fairly sober personality, yet curious and anxious to engage and impress. But, nevertheless, a flirt and a lady's man!" David had seen me in a way I would have been happy to have seen myself. I had seen David as a flirt and lady's man. What does anyone really know?

People often imagine the past being different from what it was. What had begun as a search for David had become a revelation of myself. It has been said that every man has a sense of himself, but that the gap between how he sees himself and how the outside world views him can be chasmic. Yet, after reading his words and hearing his widow's, I came to more fully value myself—thanks to a deceased friend.

On September 16, I boarded British Air Flight #173 to New York, the city of eight million stories. Mid-flight, David spoke to me. He said, with all the timbre and resonance I had come to know in his voice: "You never know what anyone else is thinking."

He had told me the same one night at Shepard's, but, he had added, "you can often tell what they feel."

Acknowledgements

I wish to thank Vicky Craver, and, of course, David.

I will always appreciate John Riley's kindness and punctuality.

I love with all my heart my dear Maura and my son and daughters, who have learned I'm anything but perfect, but that I've tried my best to be for them the father I wish had been around for me.

And, importantly, my belated thanks—and apologies—to the many dedicated teachers, vice principals, truant officers, and school crosswalk monitors who cared more about me than I perhaps did myself. I want them to know I did learn something.

CPSIA information can be obtained
at www.ICGtesting.com
Printed in the USA
FSHW010210131118
53740FS